D0759891

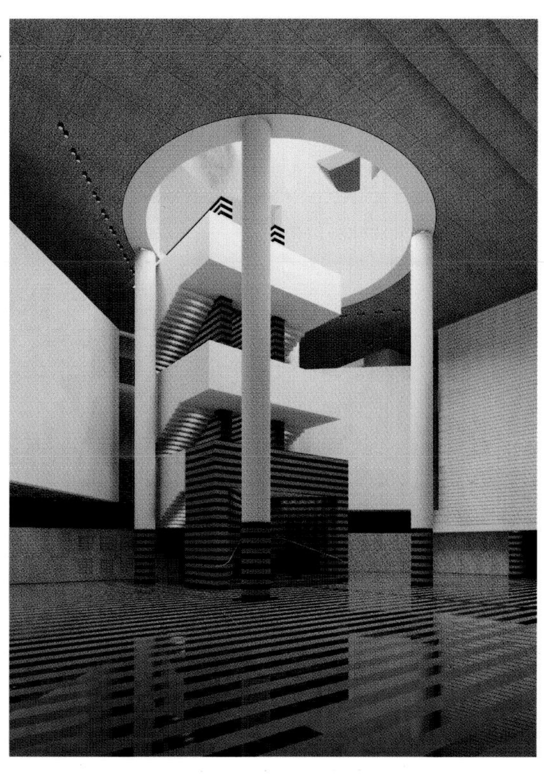

HYPER-REALISTIC

COMPUTER GENERATED ARCHITECTURAL RENDERINGS

McGraw-Hill
New York • Washington D.C. • San Francisco • Montreal • Toronto

COMPUTER GENERATED
ARCHITECTURAL RENDERINGS

HYPER-REALISTIC

Oscar Riera Ojeda   Lucas H. Guerra

ABOVE: *Banyoles Hotel Lobby. Peter Eisenman Architects. Rendered by David Johnson*

First published in the United States of America by:
McGraw Hill

First published in Germany by:
NIPPAN
Nippon Shuppan Hanbai
Deutschland GmbH
Krefelder Str. 85
D-40549 Düsseldorf
Telephone: (0211) 5048089
Fax: (0211) 5049326

All other distribution:
Rockport Publishers
Rockport, Massachusetts

ISBN 0-07-856635-5

10 9 8 7 6 5 4 3 2 1

Printed in Hong Kong

Page 1: San Francisco Museum of Modern Art. Mario Botta, architect. Rendering by Mieczyslaw Boryslawski / View by View, Inc. San Francisco, rendered using the Lightscape Visualization System. End Papers: Concrete Wall from Hurva Synagogue, Jerusalem, Israel. Louis I. Kahn, architect. Rendering by Kent Larson.

Graphic Design: Lucas H. Guerra
Oscar Riera Ojeda

Contents

Just the Beginning of The Change

Oscar Riera Ojeda

Historically, the turn of a century has always been a period marked by enormous anxiety and a search for change. At the end of one century and the beginning of the next, new geopolitical and economic configurations emerge, with their consequent influences upon art and society. Now only four years before the new millennium, a powerful current of innovation appears to flow in the most traditional of the arts: architecture. The dazzling change that I perceive will no doubt transcend far beyond mere cosmetic, linguistic, or technological issues.

We could pose several questions concerning the gestation of this advance. Is it possible that a new mode of representation can be a decisive factor in architecture's radical change? At first, this may appear to be wild conjecture. But, if alternative methods of expressing our creative imagination have profound effects upon its realization, the concept would not appear to be so wild. We are rekindling an ancient supposition: that every technological advance is accompanied by a new structure of thought.

If we analyze the popular resistance to Modern architecture (or any other significant movement in architecture) it appears that one of the reasons for this resistance was in Modern architecture's archaic and deficient representation. Gradual construction was the tool of Modernism's diffusion. But had it been possible to use a more effective medium to communicate its principles and ideas, its history would surely have been different. The wishes of Le Corbusier to develop architecture on a par with (or perhaps ahead of) the products of science and industry might have been realized, with a clearer and more direct crystallization of his notions of space.

In expressing an avant garde ideal through traditional means, sooner or later we would arrive at its limitations, with the consequent loss of force and consistency of the message. We have learned this from history, and it corresponds to the growing interest to find the appropriate tool to give form to our new ideas.

With the massive use of computers in architecture, everyone quickly assumed that "the solution" was at hand. However, it has taken several years for the digital age to produce, among other things, an appropriate way to configure architectural space. But now that we have begun to understand its essence, the connecting thread among idea, development, and construction seems to be established, exploiting every technological advance that permits improved visualization. What just a few years ago was a hesitation to use three-dimensional computer renderings has become an veritable fury. Architectural offices began to phase out the hiring of freelance computer artists or illustrators to design these superrealistic images, in favor of incorporating in-house personnel and technology that would permit this tangible method of visualization. What had been an option that provoked little confidence, that was scorned and undervalued, has today become practically indispensable.

In the three-and-a-half years of compiling this book, I recall with amazement and with delight how the earliest images created by the architectural firms represented here improved in only a matter of months from a caricaturesque quality, to their superrealistic photographic appearance today. How different our perception of the unreal is, when we become conscious of the fact that today imagination itself can be represented as an "authentic" part of reality, no longer as if in a dream, or an idea vaguely roaming in the mind of its creator.

Let us imagine that our vision of an nonexistent building might be shown in photographs, video, or some other digital form, as if it were already constructed, and that it might be possible for us to stroll through it and alter its conditions — a sort of tour through Virtual Reality. We could visualize, in an unlimited way, its interior and exterior from virtually any angle, from diverse heights and points of view, and experience it under various atmospheric and luminal conditions. Proceeding on our tour, it would

LEFT AND ABOVE: *THREE IMAGES OF THE SAITAMA ARENA IN JAPAN, DESIGNED BY ARATA ISOZAKI & ASSOCIATES, RENDERED BY THE CAD CENTER CORPORATION (TOKYO). ISOZAKI IS ONE OF THE ARCHITECTS WHO HAS MANAGED TO EXPLOIT THE POWER OF THESE IMAGES, WITHOUT ALTERING THE SPIRIT AND LANGUAGE THAT HAVE CHARACTERIZED HIS WORK IN THE PAST.*

ABOVE: *Lobby of the Shanghai Stock Exchange in Shanghai, China, by Kaplan McLaughlin Diaz. Such superrealist representation of projects is but the first step that the digital revolution is developing, in its search for a more complete and continuous experi-*

ENCE OF SPACE. CAPTURING THE ESSENCE OF LIFE AND MOVEMENT IS ONLY ONE OF THE GOALS OF THIS NEW METHOD OF VISUALIZATION FOR OUR CREATIVE IMAGINATION, WHOSE OBJECTIVE IS TO EXCITE AND ALLOW THE USE OF ALL FIVE SENSES.

THIS SPREAD: *views of the Houston Project, a private house and studio on a corner site in what is known as midtown – an area that stretches 12 blocks from Houston's downtown to Mies van der Rohe's Museum of Fine Arts, at the edge of Herman Park. Designed in 1994 by the architect Michael Bell, this project intends, by using a full sequence of computer renderings, to clearly express both "movements" present in the house: the mobile subject and the stress/strains/torsions of matter. The project was an explicit attempt to work on a kind of molecular activity in the walls as a subject activity.*

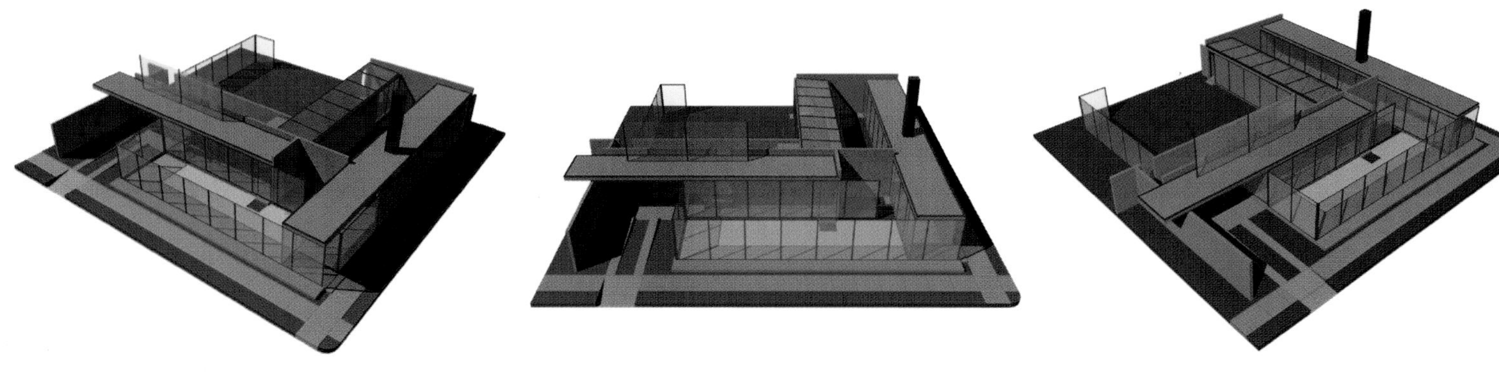

be possible for us to change the furnishings; alter the form, size, or position of any element, such as a door or a window; or to modify colors or materials. We could perhaps go even further, and utilize all of our senses. We could manipulate the materials that compose our imaginary edifice, open a window and smell the aroma of the vegetation that envelops it, or listen to the sound of the birds in the neighborhood, or of breaking waves, if our supposed building was near the seashore.

For those architects focused on the academic exercise of designing architecture only in terms of plan, section, and elevation, this new way of representing a project would finally allow them to imagine its most minute detail. But even more important is the demand it puts upon its creators to fantasize about the possible conditions of life that will reign over the created object.

Today, to experience unbuilt architecture to this hyperrealistic degree appears to be a dream. However, it is a new reality that is not more prevalent only because of time and production costs. But I have no doubt about its rapid dissemination, and that a profound change in communicating time and space has begun. Its intrinsic value is the possibility to exploit and develop a new architecture that reflects our present spirit. Only a few years ago, the appropriate form of expressing all of its principles did not exist.

The exquisite and rigorous renderings in this book, produced by some of the most important architectural firms in the world, and also by small studios of young architects, document the beginnings of this "new wave." Beyond compiling a "de mode" way of representing architecture, Hyper-Realistic Computer Generated Architectural Renderings constitutes one of the first attempts to manifest the diverse effects that the use and development of this technology will have on architecture's future course. These new tools pave the way for us.

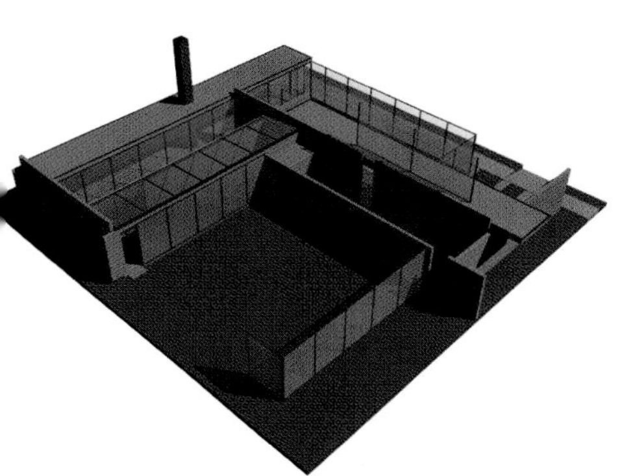

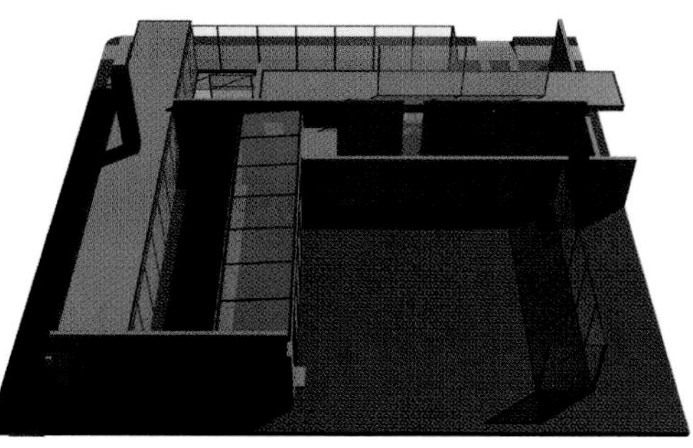

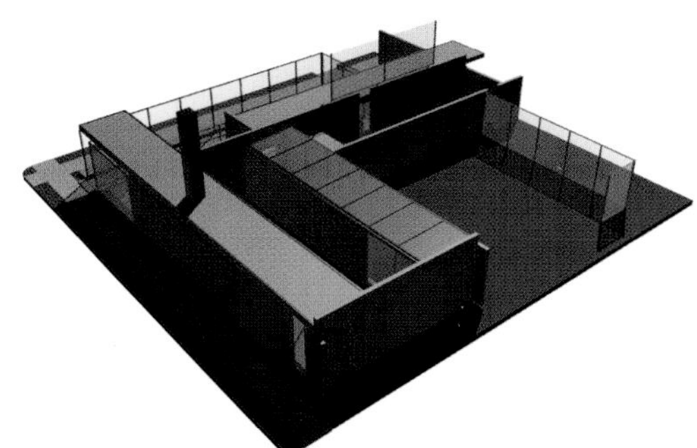

A.C.–after computer–Era

Lucas H. Guerra

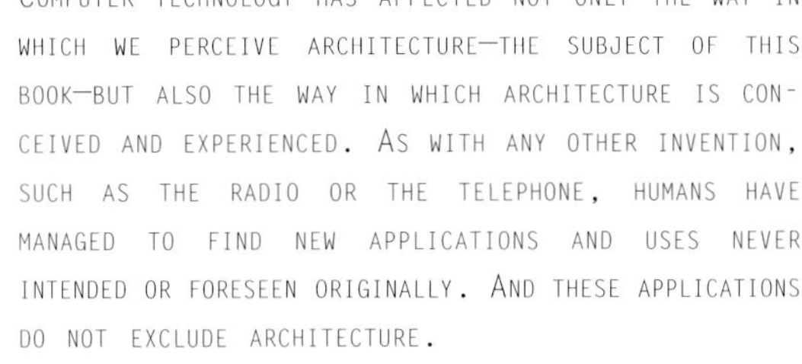

Computer technology has affected not only the way in which we perceive architecture—the subject of this book—but also the way in which architecture is conceived and experienced. As with any other invention, such as the radio or the telephone, humans have managed to find new applications and uses never intended or foreseen originally. And these applications do not exclude architecture.

I have worked extensively with many architects and have personally experienced the implementation of the computer in architectural practice. Originally used for CAD applications, computers gradually became part of the design process and eventually came to play a major role in the presentation of architecture through computer-generated renderings.

Three years ago, when I began research for this book, few offices were using this technology strictly as a CAD tool. Others had not yet incorporated computers into their architectural practice. In the past few years I have witnessed the growth of this technology in offices that had a conservative design process, but who were willing to reshape it in order to use the computer.

Computers have not only become important tools in almost every practice, but have gradually become familiar objects in our workplaces as well as in our homes. The personal computing revolution of the 1970s and '80s made available fast and relatively inexpensive technology to produce digital imagery. Today we can sit clients in front of a computer screen and take them around the "site" on a walk-through animation, allowing them to not only perceive but also to experience architecture in a new realistic manner. As this publication portrays, we create computer-generated environments that we can interactively explore as "virtual reality," soon to be tangible.

If we looking back into history and analyze events that served as this century's turning points, we may understand how we became immersed in this technological avalanche, with an impact and magnitude never seen before.

Back in the beginning of this century, 1903 to be exact, the Wright Brothers successfully flew a little over a hundred meters skimming the face of the earth. This was, indeed, a major turning point in history. But only 66 years later (within a single lifetime of experience) man stepped on the surface of the moon, looking back at planet Earth and realizing that together, with television and telecommunications, this planet was already getting smaller.

By 1943 computers were already a part of our history. With names such as "Electronic Delay Variable Automatic Computer" and "Electronic Integrator Numerator and Analyzer." They stretched 51 feet long, weighed five tons, and consisted of 4,000 tubes and 10,000 crystal diodes with a clock speed of 100 Khz. A decade later, a so-called "computer" still occupied 25,000 square feet. This rate of change seems terribly slow compared to the computer development today.

Today we familiarly call them Macs, PCs or SGs. Some litter our desks, replacing the old wheel-based Rolodex and our appointment book. Some we carry in our briefcases, so we can work while we're on the road. Computers change virtually week-by-week, becoming more powerful and faster, while we try to stay up to date with new models and devices.

Major advances characterize this century and I believe that by the year 2000—right around the corner—when we appraise the events that shaped this century, we will be doing it in binary form and will come to recognize the computer as the machine that changed the world.

Computers are no longer viewed as a medium just to store information or create fancy pie-charts. They went further than becoming the medium to create digital imagery, eventually morphing into the medium for a world wide web of communication. We could philosophically conceptualize the Internet as a world wide, virtual or pseudo-community in which we are citizens, belonging to a geographical or digital neighborhood called site.

Computers have become the infrastructure of the Internet, which grows at an amazing 25 percent a month. It is hard to be unaware of the Internet revolution as terms such as the "Net," "Cyberspace," or "Multimedia" have unconsciously become part of our everyday vocabulary. I personally believe the Internet to be one of the most important technological innovations happening right now—since my mind cannot begin to wonder what kind of technological achievements will take place a mere five years from now.

Looking into the future, I would say we are the pioneers in exploring the new domains of technology, the witnesses of a new "electronic social revolution." As the title of this essay tries to convey we are living in a new digital era. The future applications to this new technologies leave me entangled into a "web" of thoughts. I hope they are productive ones.

The research for this essay was done entirely on the World Wide Web. A total of 86 pages of specific information was retrieved from the web in around 40 minutes, with the stroke of only six keywords.

Opposite Page: *(top) Agnes Etherington Art Centre, Competition Entry, Ontario, Canada. (bottom) IBM Canada Ltd., Toronto, Canada*
This Page: *(top) Faculty of Business Management, University of Toronto, Competition Entry, Ontario, Canada. (bottom) Jerusalem City Hall Complex, Jerusalem, Israel*
The design, 3D models and computer renderings of these super-realistic virtual spaces were created by A.J. Diamond, Donald Schmitt and Company, Architect. The software used was—radiosity-based—Lightscape Visualization System.

New Technologies, Lost Values

Kent Larson

Part of the so-called "digital revolution" is a tendency to see these new technologies as the means to reclaim values held prior to the industrial revolution.

Three recent examples come to mind: Vice President Al Gore, dubbed by the New York Times as the "President of the Commonwealth of Cyberspace," suggests widespread access to the Internet will help return us to the ideals of Jeffersonian democracy; House Speaker Newt Gingrich proposes that the poor receive subsidized laptop computers to allow participation in electronic town meetings; Wired magazine, the self appointed mouthpiece of the digital revolution, argues that the network of medieval monasteries formed the original internet - that the great freedom of individual expression enjoyed by pre-Gutenberg writers and artists, later lost with the control of commercial publishing houses, has now been reclaimed by desktop publishing and the uncensored and immediate outlets like the World Wide Web.

Admittedly, some of this is a bit of a stretch. Digital technology is a new development with little in the past to guide us as to how our lives and culture will be altered. We only have to look at the many new books by the techno-pundits to see a lack of consensus. Nicholas Negroponte of the MIT Media Lab has a best seller Being Digital, which the New York Times summarizes as arguing that new technology changes everything for the better. Clifford Stoll's new book, Silicon Snake Oil, has a less optimistic message as is clear by the title.

In architecture, however, this most modern of technologies does seem to offer the possibility of allowing us to reclaim certain lost values of the past.

Two hundred and fifty years ago, Piranesi published his powerful Carceri etchings of dark prisons, which have influenced how architects think of space ever since their publication. These are perceptual images of the highest order. Less well known are Piranesi's meticulous analytical/conceptual images. In his Della Magnificenza ed Architettura d Romani, for example, are beautifully organized montages of plan, isometric, section, details, and elevations, as Modern in their intention as any of the 20th Century. Piranesi was skilled at selecting the appropriate graphic tool for the task - conceptual images to convey information impossible to perceive in perspective, perspective images to communicate the experience of space impossible to view in plan/section/isometric projections, and nonaxial distortions of space carefully contrived to elicit a particular, often uncomfortable and disorienting response. Likewise, the work of successors to Piranesi such as Ledoux, Boullee, and John Soane (or rather John Gandy, who rendered Soane's work) all exhibit a balance of conceptual projections to explain architectural ideas, with perspective views to allow the viewer to experience space.

The representational rendering of architectural space has gradually diminished since the 1920s with the Modernist preoccupation with analytical images and disdain of the perceptual. A bias developed against "subjective" work that reproduces an individual view of space. Along with detail and ornament, early Modernists abandoned the representational graphic techniques for more abstract imagery. Mies van der Rohe and his contemporaries continued to use the perspective to explore basic form, but they used it in a conceptual way - through graphic photo-montage or minimalist line drawings. Corbusier's little perspective line drawings of his unbuilt Palace of the Soviets are wonderful images, but it is exceedingly difficult to understand from these sketches how the building would actually have been experienced.

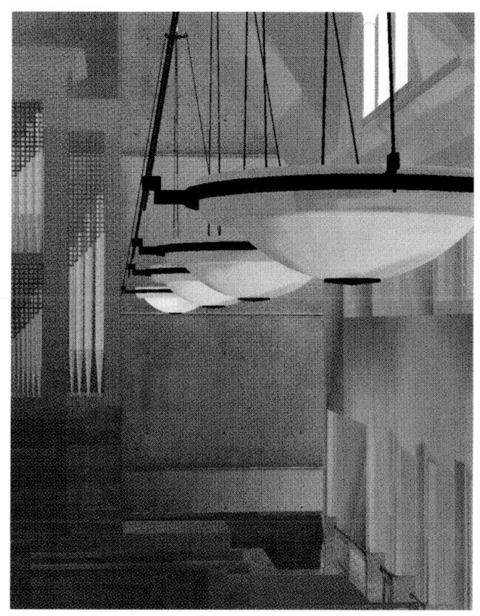

Later Modernists often abandoned even the abstract use of perspective as a viable tool. Scarpa and Kahn, although concerned with crafting interior space, light, and materials, produced few perspective studies to communicate these qualities. The meticulously line-textured perspectives of Paul Rudolph are as close as architects of this period come to an 18th-century draftsman's concern for communicating the experience of space. More recently, one can find both ideological rationalizations and practical explanations for this devaluation of the perspective. Architects of the past 20 or so years have usually preferred complexity, irony, and obfuscation to clarity. Representational images do not support these ideals. Not surprisingly, many buildings of this period lack qualities of space and light sufficient to be effectively presented with three-dimensional media, as the uninspiring photographs (perspective views) of the built space confirm. Concurrent with this has been a decline in the ability of architects to draw in three dimensions. It is disappointing to find that many young architects think mainly in two dimensions, and many from even the best schools are unable to sketch in perspective. In fact, instructors often actively discourage the use of perspective as a study tool. One need only walk through the studios of Harvard, Yale, and Columbia to find an aversion to the representational - to see that abstracted imagery is preferred to representations which conform to the laws of optics. The communication of the idea is all-important - the experience of its realization receives little attention.

This lack of skill with the production of perceptual images has lead to the development of a cottage industry of professional renderers outside of the architectural profession to produce those alien and artistically dubious perspectives demanded by clients and review boards so that lay people can actually understand a proposal.

Enter sophisticated computer graphics at the very end of the 20th century. We are now at the stage where any image can be created digitally. We can produce analytical images as dense, layered, and obscure as any Deconstructivist, or as meticulous as a Beaux Arts section/perspective, or as graphic and saturated as a silkscreen. Complex structures can be studied using dynamic sections as with a CAT scan. Fragments can be filtered, doctored, montaged, overlaid, and processed into non-linear hypermedia assemblies of film, stills, and audio. Even if the subtle line of a pencil sketch cannot be replicated (who would want to?), we can scan, manipulate, and combine the work of traditional media with unprecedented ease. We can also create perceptual studies as convincingly realistic as any photograph or film. Actual materials, with all of their imperfections and rich variety, can be photographed, scaled, and applied to surfaces of a model. We can prepare physically accurate simulations of light - even down to the use of goniometric diagrams to describe the precise dispersion from a specific downlight, penumbra and all. The path of sunlight throughout a day or season can be viewed interactively. A single digital model can be used for all our purposes - outputted as plan, elevation, section, axonometric, and perspective, even if considerable effort is required to tailor a database to produce the intended result. These new tools are now affordable enough for architects to acquire, and accessible enough for them to actually use. If this technology has so much potential, why is there relatively little digital work of quality in the architectural profession?

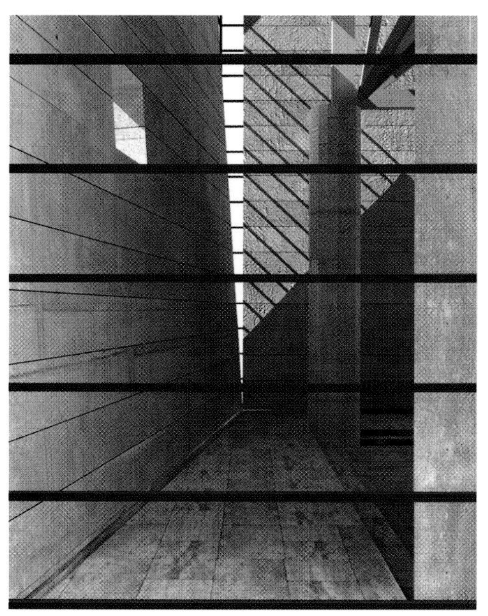

The barriers to the use of these new tools are more cultural and artistic than technological. It is interesting to note that in spite of the marvelous creative possibilities of this technology, few architects have gone beyond the predictable use of the standard low-fidelity output of off-the-shelf low-tech tools. Most attempts to use digital tools in architecture have been for client presentations where the crude, sterile perspective constructs are far less satisfying than the pastel commercial images of the renderer-for-hire they are intended to replace. Computer graphic work of architecture to date has been a largely uncomfortable muddle of the perceptual and the conceptual - neither analytical images which explain ideas, nor perceptual images which convincingly communicate space.

Architecture is a more conservative profession than most would like to admit. Unworkable and inefficient habits die slowly, and new methods are slow to be incorporated and perfected. Whereas science and industrial design quickly adopted digital technologies, the profession of architecture has only begun to explore the vast potential of these new tools. There are still far too few senior architects who understand the implications and potential of working digitally, and fewer still who can personally do it.

But there are signs that this is rapidly changing. The lost art of communicating the experience of architecture is being developed again by a new generation of designers. This will, one hopes, lead to a restoration of balance between the conceptual and perceptual as was found in the work of the 18th century, and mitigate the effects of a degradation of drawing skills. A clear advantage to the use of computer graphics in architecture is that digital representations, in both two and three dimensions, can be created from a fully three-dimensional model. These tools require that a building be precisely described in space, which makes it difficult to fall back on merely two-dimensional graphic imagery, however compelling.

Used in conjunction with more schematic physical models, this technology seems to force architects to think more clearly in three dimensions and gain a better understanding of connections and form. It has also permitted the visualization of complex shapes impractical to describe with conventional media. That the technology has all too often led to the indiscriminate production of unartful material does not diminish its potential.

Architects with greater skill and vision are just now beginning to adopt computer graphics, permitting a return to a more hands-on involvement in the design and presentation process. As young architects raised on Nintendo become confident designers, they will again be able to personally develop ideas and craft presentations without depending on apprentices to painstakingly craft models and drawings by hand using traditional media.

We are coming full circle: Digital perspective images are finding their way into the work of art-star architects who formerly shunned all but the most abstract representations. Digital tools designed originally for the hyperrealistic perspective rendering of light and materials are also being used to craft complex, abstract, non-representational presentations of the idea.

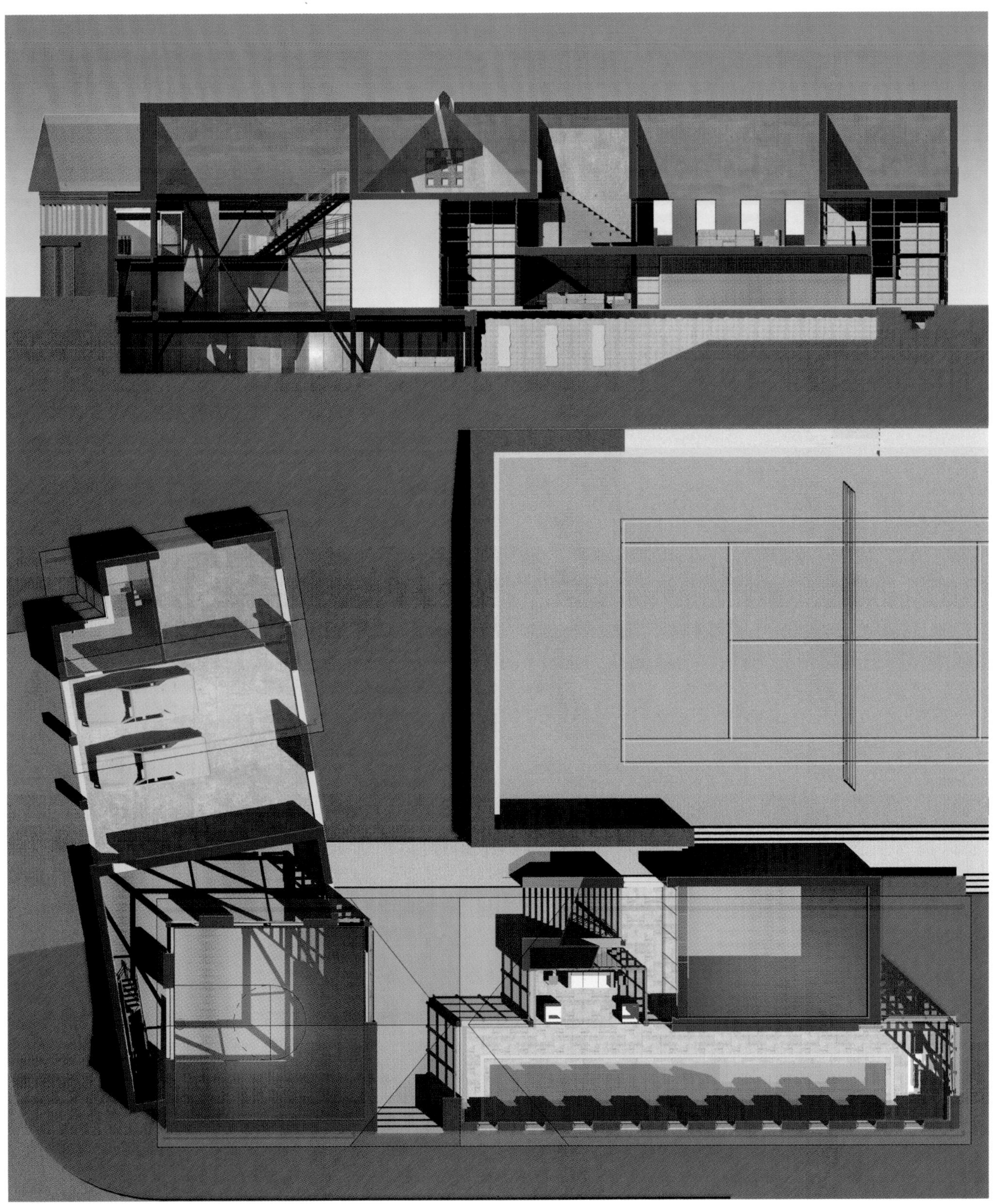

Above: *Private Sports Facility, Southampton, New York, Peter L. Gluck and Partners, architect, rendered by Kent Larson.*
Opposite Page: *House in Ridgefield, Connecticut. Kent Larson, Architect PC. An indoor pool links the residence and offices of a professional couple. The site is wooded and secluded, with views to a private lake. The interior finishes are tinted plaster and mahogany doors and windows. These images are rendered by Kent Larson as design development studies of the play of natural light.*

ARCHITECTURAL OFFICES

Kohn Pedersen Fox Associates PC

Rafael Viñoly Architects

Cesar Pelli & Associates

Machado & Silvetti Associates

Estudio Becker-Ferrari

Office dA

Skidmore, Owings & Merrill

Gwathmey Siegel & Associates

Hellmuth, Obata + Kassabaum

Bohlin Cywinski Jackson Architects

ADD Inc

Peter L. Gluck & Partners

Cross Point.
Cambridge, Massachusetts
ADD Inc
Rendering by Anthony Tan

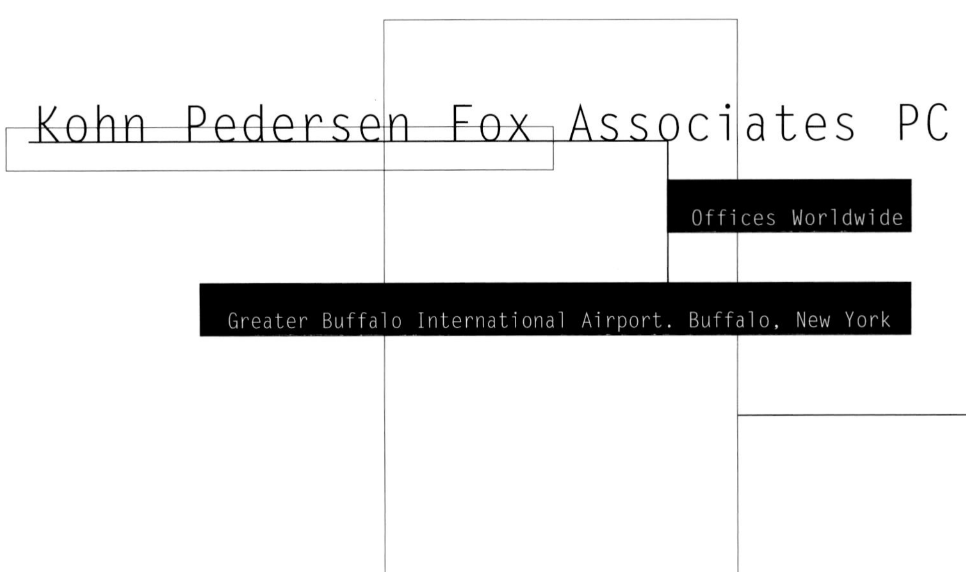

Kohn Pedersen Fox offers full architecture, master planning, space planning, programming and building analysis services. The firm's work in the United States has earned KPF recognition as one of the most respected architectural firms in the country. With offices in New York, London, Tokyo, and Berlin, and an increasing number of projects in countries such as the Philippines, Japan, Korea, Indonesia, Singapore, China, Australia, Cyprus, Chile, England, Germany, France, Canada, and Scotland, the firm's reputation is growing. KPF consists of eight partners, fifteen senior associate partners, and seventeen associate partners - supported by a professional and technical staff of one hundred and thirty.

The Use of Computers at Kohn Pedersen Fox Associates PC

The philosophy guiding the design process at KPF is one of collaboration; collaboration within the design team, with outside consultants, and ultimately with clients. We believe that all voices participating in this design process should be equally heard. At KPF, we use computer capabilities in an equally collaborative way. The addition of computer drafting, 3-D modeling and rendering does not preclude traditional forms of representation and investigation, rather it is an equal participant with these tools in the overall design process. A 3-D computer model may help resolve complex geometry, offer multivalent views of the same form, and therefore increase the ability to study more design options within a shorter time frame. Yet the construction of the virtual model with the computer does not supplant the construction of the physical scale model. Instead it informs that construction to a more complete and realizable scale, particularly those designs of a complex geometric nature.

The computer allows for a greater understanding of the collision, intersection, overlap, or separation of not only formal geometric properties, but of the integral building systems. With the

DESIGN OF THE GREATER BUFFALO INTERNATIONAL AIRPORT IT WAS NECESSARY TO GENERATE A STRUCTURAL MODEL OF THE BUILDING CONCURRENT WITH ITS ARCHITECTURAL, VOLUMETRIC ENCLOSURE TO VERIFY RESOLUTION OF THE TWISTING, WARPED, AND CURVED SURFACES THAT DESCRIBE THE ROOF PLANES. THE DEGREE TO WHICH THE COMPUTER CAN RENDER PERSPECTIVE DRAWINGS AND MODELS TO REPRESENT THE REALITY OF MATERIAL, LIGHTING, OR BACKGROUND IS LESS A PART OF THE DESIGN PROCESS THAN ITS ABILITY TO ABSTRACT THE RELATIONSHIP OF ARCHITECTURAL ELEMENTS. IT IS THESE SPATIAL RELATIONSHIPS AND FORMAL COMPOSITIONS WE SEEK TO RESOLVE WITH THE COMPUTER.

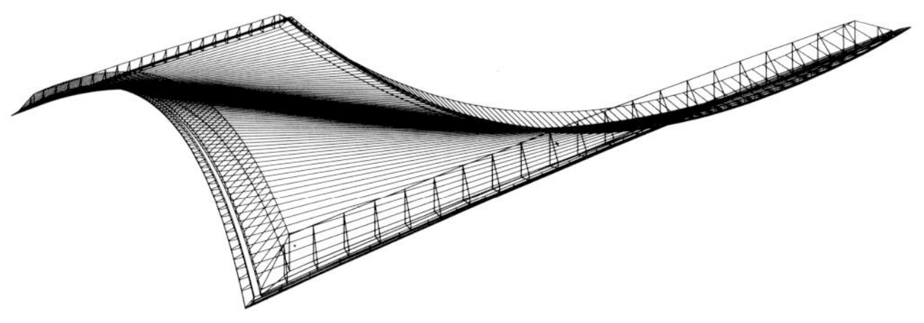

SUBSEQUENT VIEWING OF THE 3-D COMPUTER MODEL OF THE BUFFALO AIRPORT DESIGN FROM MULTIPLE VANTAGE POINTS PROVIDED A MORE SPECIFIC AND PRECISE PLATFORM FOR THE CREATION OF BUILDING SECTION AND ELEVATION DRAWINGS. TWO-DIMENSIONAL EXPORT FILES FROM THE THREE-DIMENSIONAL MODEL ENSURE THE ACCURACY OF OBLIQUE VIEWS OF THE COMPLEX SHAPES INTEGRAL TO THE DESIGN. THE DESIGN TEAM IS THEN ABLE TO CREATE CONSTRUCTION DOCUMENTS BASED UPON THE GEOMETRIC ENCLOSURE DESCRIBED BY THE 3-D COMPUTER MODEL OF THE ENTIRE TERMINAL.

MANY OF KPF'S RECENT PROJECTS HAVE BEEN FOR GOVERNMENTAL AGENCIES, SUCH AS THE GSA. INCREASINGLY, THESE CONTRACTS REQUIRE THAT CONSTRUCTION DOCUMENTS BE DONE ON COMPUTER; IN THE CASE OF THE BUFFALO AIRPORT ALL DOCUMENTATION HAD TO BE COMPUTER-BASED. THE DEGREE OF ACCURACY WITH WHICH WE CAN COMMUNICATE BETWEEN CLIENT AND CONSULTANT IS STRENGTHENED WITHIN THE COMPUTER ENVIRONMENT, NOT ONLY WITH CONSTRUCTION DRAWINGS, BUT ALSO WITH THE MODELS AND PERSPECTIVES CREATED FOR DESIGN RESOLUTION. THE COMPUTER HAS BECOME AS VALUABLE A TOOL IN THE DESIGN PROCESS AS IT HAS BECOME WITH THE PRODUCTION PROCESS.

ABOVE: *EXTERIOR VIEW OF THE GREATER BUFFALO INTERNATIONAL AIRPORT AND WIREFRAME RENDERING OF ROOF.*

Kohn Pedersen Fox Associates PC

renderer

Advanced Media Design

Greater Buffalo International Airport

Buffalo, New York

The Greater Buffalo International Airport project has several parallel goals. First, to consolidate an outdated two-terminal facility into one modern terminal housing all airlines. Second, to enhance passenger convenience and comfort from automobile approach to aircraft departure. And finally, to establish a comprehensive gateway image for both the city of Buffalo and the western New York region.

The site is 10 miles east of downtown Buffalo, within the context of a flat, suburban landscape defined by strip highway development. Currently there exist two terminals originally dating from 1939, with additions and expansions through 1976. A large surface parking lot with minimal landscaping connects these separate buildings. A new control tower serving one major and one minor crosswind runway is located a half-mile east of the terminals. The program calls for the construction of a new two-level terminal, landscaped loop roadway system, a two-level parking garage for 1,300 cars, and surface parking lots for an additional 1,100 cars.

The design for the airport evolved from an investigation of planning principles and shifting volumetric properties in response to the experience of the passenger or visitor. For passenger convenience and accessibility, the building provides a distinct sequencing of activities as one moves from automobile to aircraft. To further articulate that experience in movement, a series of interpenetrating forms represent each of the terminal's major public spaces: ticketing hall, concessions link, and departures concourse. Passengers are led from ticketing check-in to flight take-off through a variety of distinct volumetric experiences.

The design employs gently curving forms in both plan and section to reflect the tension between the statics of structure and the excitement of flight. The arching metal roofs appear poised for flight. Furthermore, the terminal's changing massing and sectional characteristics reflect the process of spatial compression and expansion inherent to jet travel: distance contracts, boundaries of experience extend, and time constantly shifts. The design explores this experience of movement from the soaring ticketing hall to the compressed fuselage of an aircraft.

The palette for the new terminal is a synthesis of aircraft technology and regional materials. The terminal is grounded in a granite base, and anchored to the runway by an arching pre-cast concrete wall that slices through the main ticketing hall, recalling the limestone outcroppings native to the Niagara district. The curvilinear roof forms are clad in stainless steel, the wall systems in a corrugated metallic silver panel and energy-efficient glazing.

USAir

AmericanAirlines

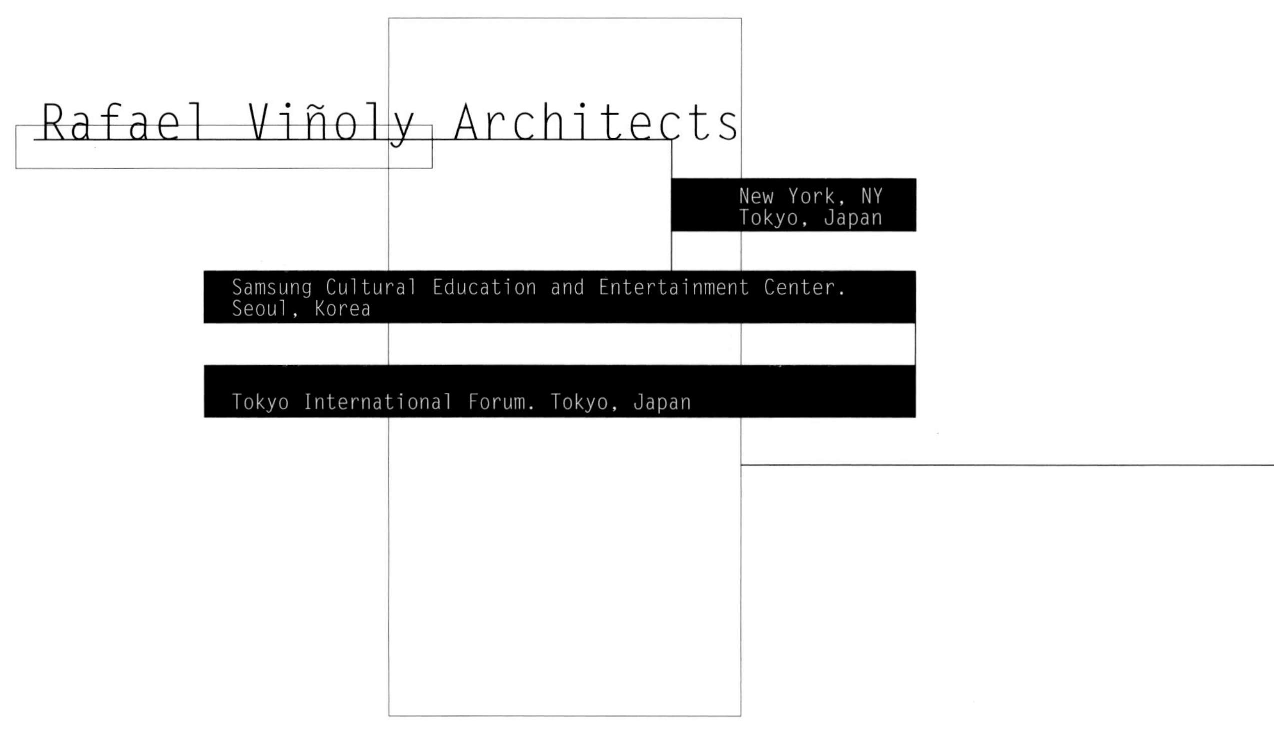

Rafael Viñoly Architects
New York, NY
Tokyo, Japan
Samsung Cultural Education and Entertainment Center. Seoul, Korea
Tokyo International Forum. Tokyo, Japan

Rafael Viñoly Architects was founded in 1982 and provides comprehensive services in building design, urban planning and interior design for new facilities, renovations, and landmark restorations. It has also successfully completed many fast-track and design/build projects.

The Use of Computers at Rafael Viñoly Architects

Rafael Viñoly Architects began using computers for two-dimensional drafting of construction documents in 1988. Between 1988 and 1990, computers were fully integrated into the office, when they were used to produce 2,000 construction documents for the Tokyo International Forum. Every architect had a workstation, and Personal Computers, Macintosh, and Silicon Graphics stations were all introduced and gradually integrated into one coordinated network. Three-dimensional modeling and rendering, initially with AutoCAD, and then, with Alias software on Silicon Graphics stations, has always been an essential utilization of the computer. In April of 1993, the firm completed its first video animation - a 14-minute walk through the Tokyo International Forum. This video took six people one year to produce and was done in-house. Every project in the office depends on the computer as a design tool, a presentation tool, a model-building tool, and a documentation tool. During construction, computers are used to monitor schedules and track shop drawing submissions.

Using a Novell local area network and PC-NFS connecting DOS-based 386 and 486 Personal Computers, Apple Macintosh computers, and Silicon Graphics stations, projects teams have access to Computer-Aided Drafting and Design (CAD) using AutoCAD, and word processing and desktop publishing programs such as Quark Xpress, Adobe Illustrator, and Adobe Photoshop. The five Silicon Graphic stations comprising the Computer Visualization/Simulation Department use the UNIX operating system to run Alias, a program with a highly sophisticated three-dimensional modeling and rendering system. Versatec laser plotters and laser printers are utilized for printing in-house. Iris printers are used for printing in color.

The office space is an open plan, organized so that project work takes place in a single area where managers and coordinators work alongside production staff, allowing for a high creativity environment,

better communication, and closer coordination. The design staff works in collaboration and in conjunction with the technical directors throughout the process, using three-dimensional models created in Alias to inform and aid in the development of each project design.

Computer modeling has been used most effectively to reinforce and enhance all other conventional tools throughout the design process. By three-dimensionally replicating the site and translating initial sketches and diagrams on the computer, ideas and concepts can be considered, tested, and developed rigorously. Computer models can reflect schematic variations and modifications cleanly, quickly, and easily when developing volumetric relationships and investigating effects of the existing site conditions and aspects, including solar orientation, views, public access and accessibility, directional flow of pedestrians, and vehicular circulation. Designers can later refine details and study specific qualities of spaces, such as materiality, color, texture, and the effects of both natural and artificial light throughout the day with reflection, refraction, and shadows.

The design staff also uses computer models as another presentation tool to convey to the client group a clear description of projects. The working process with the computer is such that while a project is "in progress," it can be readily and easily integrated in a presentation to clients. Computer modeling using simulated fly-through sequences gives clients a virtual understanding of the entire proposed environment, making the design process more accessible to the client and allowing for more interaction between designers and clients.

The computer is an invaluable tool that only strengthens the design process, diversifying and supplementing designers' critical and investigatory capabilities, and allows for more thorough and rigorous design studies. Its full creative potential has yet to be explored and discovered.

Above: *General view and interior perspective at departure and arrival hall of the Yokohama International Port Terminal*

Rafael Viñoly Architects

renderer
Rafael Viñoly Architects

Samsung Cultural Education and Entertainment Center

Seoul, Korea

The Samsung Cultural Education and Entertainment Center involves the renovation and architectural reconfiguration of an existing structure into a facility capable of addressing the goals of the projects' program. Located in the Hwashin district in downtown Seoul, the existing building is an inward-looking structure with a rather undefined architectural character. Its typical floor plate is relatively small and, consequently, the openings required to achieve a sense of spatial continuity are kept to a minimum. The structural system of the building has been altered minimally, maintaining its original integrity. Urbanistically, the public space defined by the set-back at the corner of the lot is not clearly integrated with the life of the building or the underground concourse.

The architectural solution at the core of the project is based on two guiding principles: to achieve a more public image of the building, and to transform an architectural structure into an information vehicle that facilitates education and experience.

The primary gesture of the 600,000-square-foot project attempts to transform the space left at the corner of the site into a mediating element between the public nature of the street and the activities within the building. A steel and glass canopy structure cantilevers beyond the plane of the building's facade at the top elevation of the available volume to help define this transitional public space. This zone belongs to both the city and the building, and transforms the enclosed nature of the present building into an outwardly open architectural structure. One-and-a-half-levels below grade, a similar urban connection links existing subway traffic with the building through the use of an underground urban plaza. The glass facade of the building extends to this level, serving again as the threshold between city and building.

A large, composite video-screen system located at the rear of the atrium levels forms the Information Wall. It visually connects four levels of the project and provides a source of orientation and visual reference. This element establishes not only the thematic continuity of the narrow space, but also gives it virtual depth, becoming the main advertising surface within the building.

The building extends vertically through the extrusion of the three round elements that configure the existing plan (the vertical circulation cores), transforming it into a major landmark visible at great distance. The structural reinforcement required for this addition is mitigated by the lightness of the proposed structure, which will contain only an observation platform and a panoramic restaurant. This "cloud-like" element, sitting on a tripod of structural towers, hovers over the mass of the project. At night this object seems a suspended volume of light, becoming a major landmark in the skyline of the city.

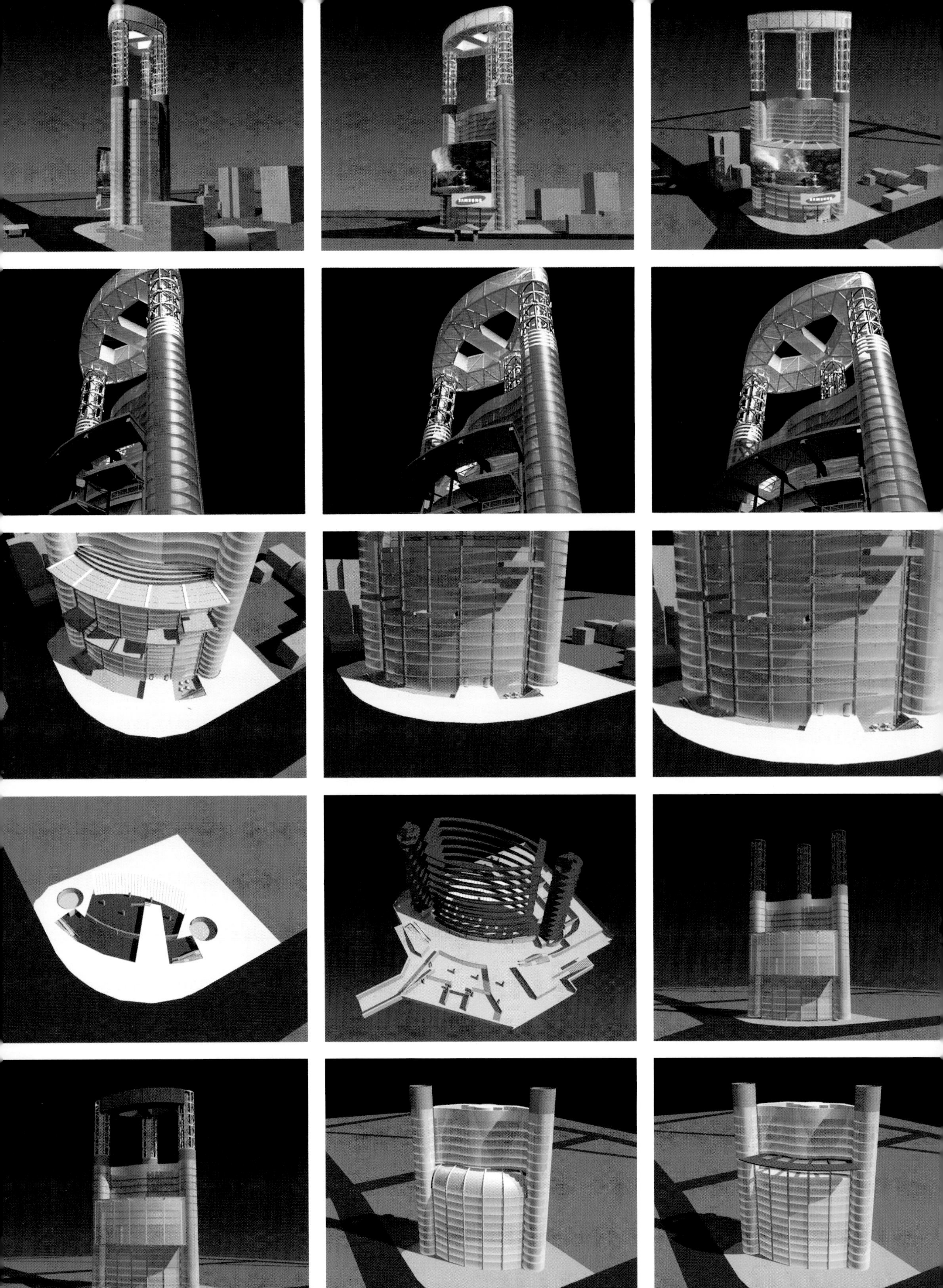
SAMSUNG
SAMSUNG

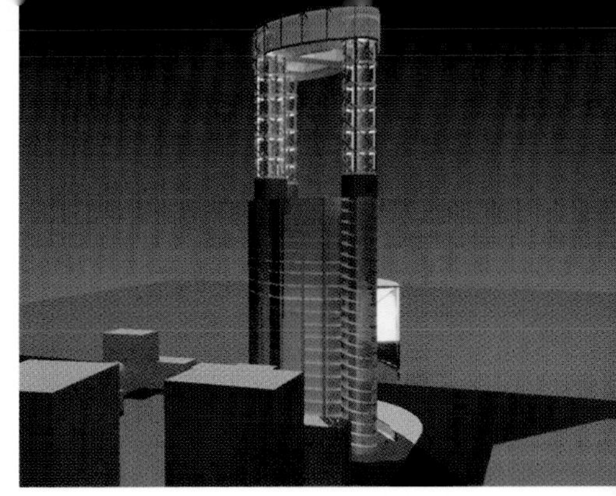
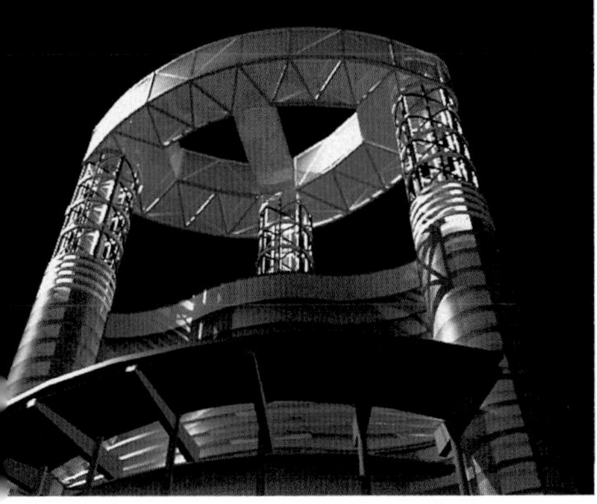

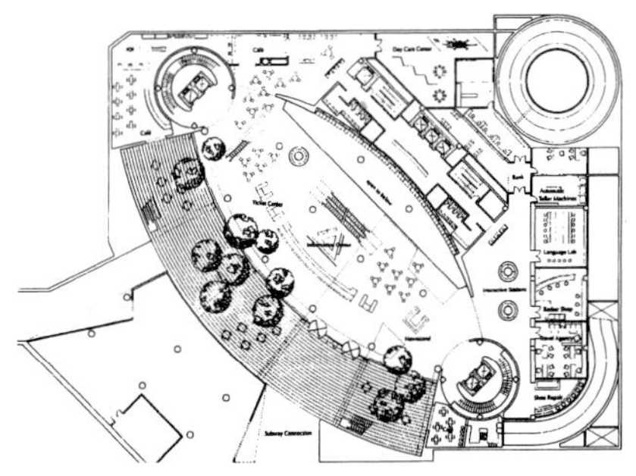

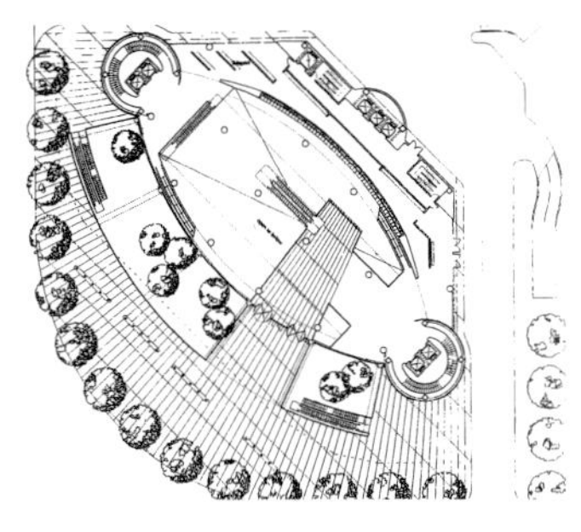

FIRST BASEMENT LEVEL-
WORLD COMMUNICATIONS PLAZA

ENTRY LEVEL-THE BRIDGE

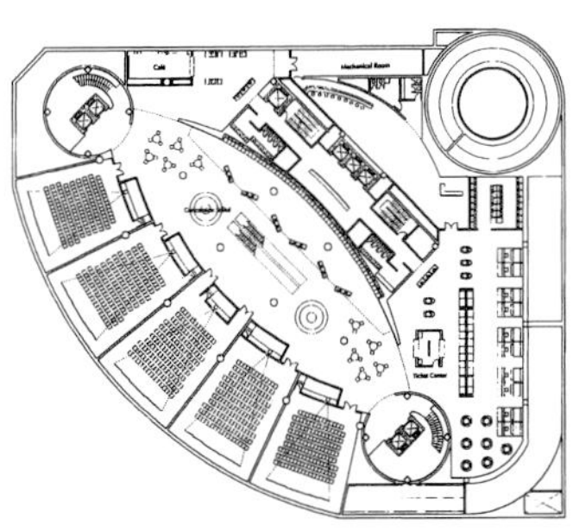
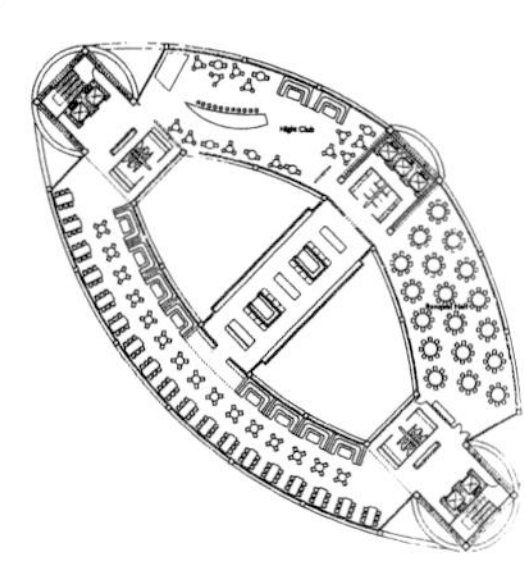

SECOND BASEMENT LEVEL-
INTERNATIONAL INTERACTION ZONE

"THE CLOUD"-NIGHT CLUB
AND OBSERVATION DECK

SAMSUNG

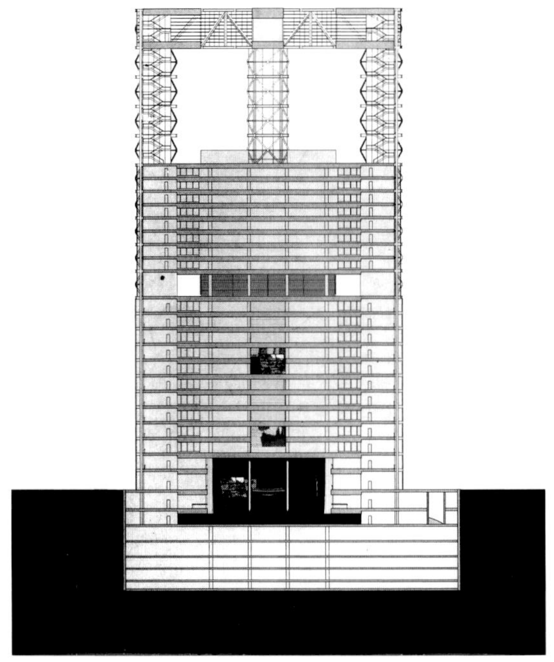

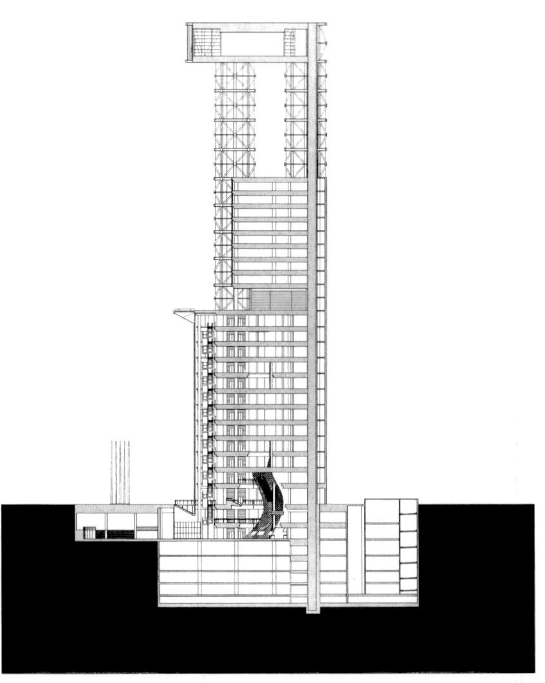

SAMSUNG

풍문고

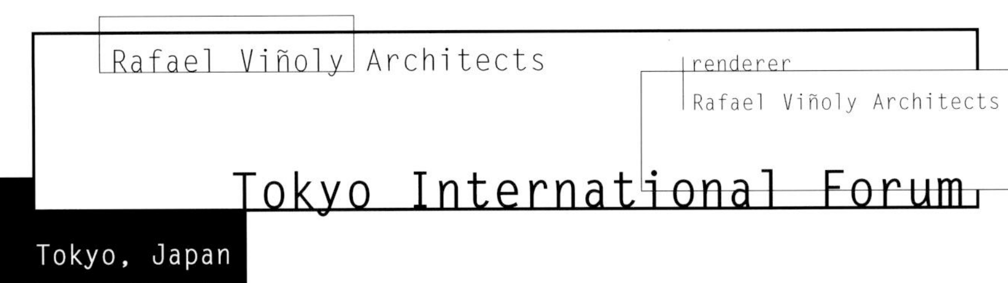

Rafael Viñoly Architects
renderer
Rafael Viñoly Architects
Tokyo International Forum
Tokyo, Japan

The Tokyo International Forum will occupy the former site of Tokyo's City Hall and City Council Building in the Marunouchi district, part of the city's central business area and adjacent to the Ginza commercial and entertainment district. The Forum site faces the outer gardens of the Imperial Palace to the west and is bounded on the east by the tracks of Japan Railways, the city's principal system of transportation. Four subway lines and two of the most heavily-used train stations, the Tokyo and Yarakucho stations, are located to the north and south of the site respectively, generating significant pedestrian traffic in the area.

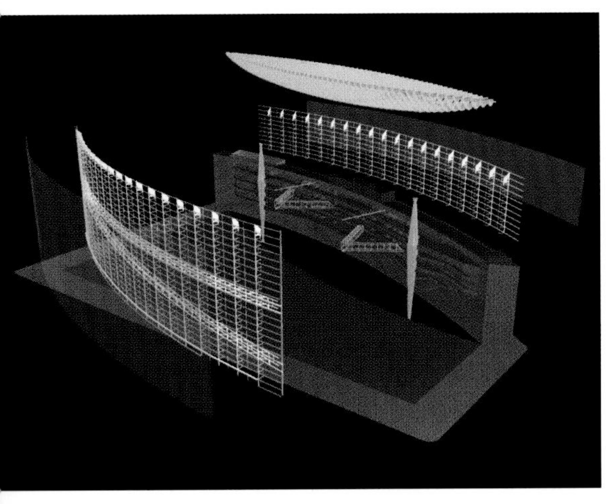

At 1.5 million square feet, the Tokyo International Forum is a unique and ambitious civic institution intended to serve as a focus of both cultural and business activities in Japan's capital. Unlike any other facility in the world, this 6.7-acre complex will accommodate dance; musical and theatrical performances; conventions and trade shows; business meetings and receptions. It will also house offices, cultural information centers, a garden, and an internationally recognized art collection. Commissioned by the Tokyo Metropolitan Government, the Forum is envisioned as a prime venue for events from around the world, as a unique center promoting open dialogue and international cultural exchange.

The Forum contains a range of performance halls, exhibition spaces, conference areas, as well as education and general information facilities. The complex is comprised of seven primary structures in addition to public spaces. A monumental Glass Hall will serve as the main reception area and signature of the project. This dramatic structure will have seven stories above ground and three underground levels. One of the most daring and imaginative structures to be built in Japan, it will consist of two intersecting glass and steel ellipses that will enclose a vast central lobby and will tie all the elements of the complex together. Two major exhibition areas will serve as spaces for receptions and trade shows. The Glass Hall will be connected to the theaters by a series of ramps and bridges. A low, curved bar building will abut the Glass Hall and will contain the Forum's Conference Center and administrative offices, restaurants, cafes and other services functions.

This public forum in the center of Tokyo has been compared to Rockefeller Center and the Piazza San Marco in Venice. The Glass Hall glowing at night in the skyline has been said to have the grandeur and civic importance of the Eiffel Tower. The Forum is a statement on the role of the institution in contemporary urban culture and, as such, it addresses the issues of permanence, openness, and civic responsibility.

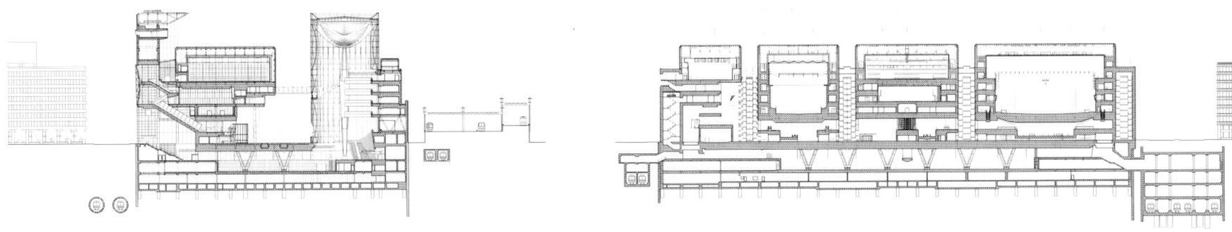

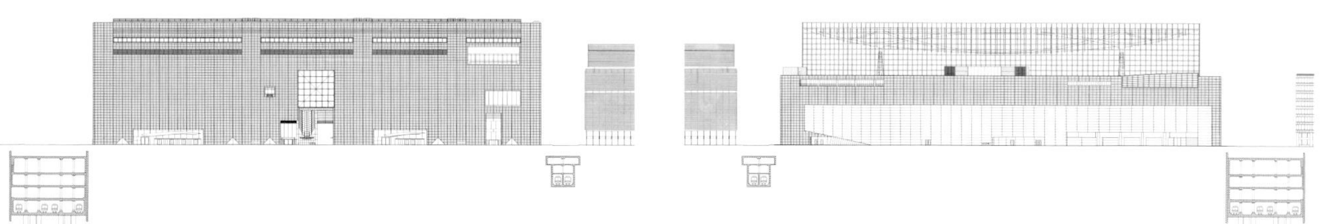

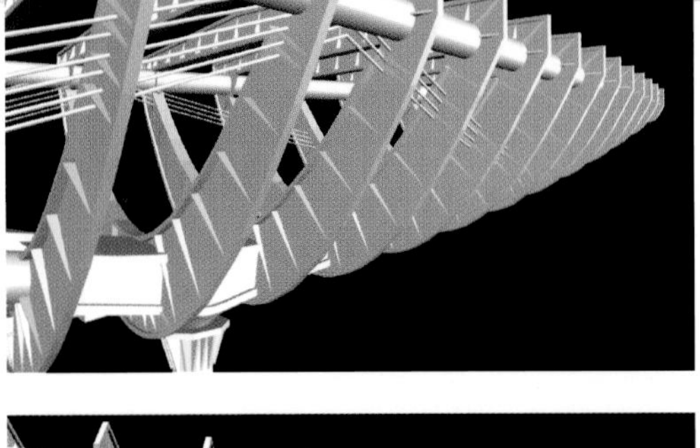

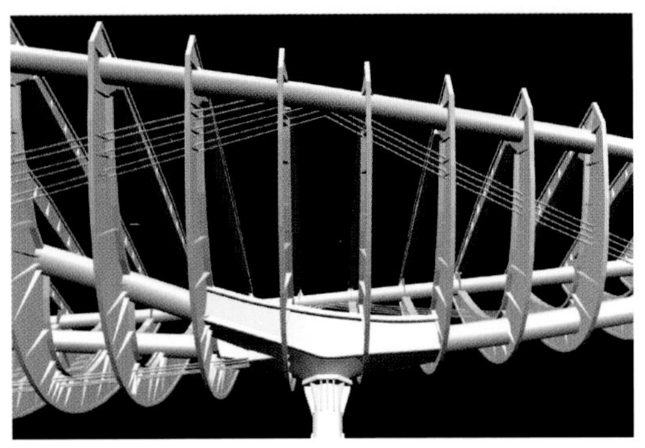

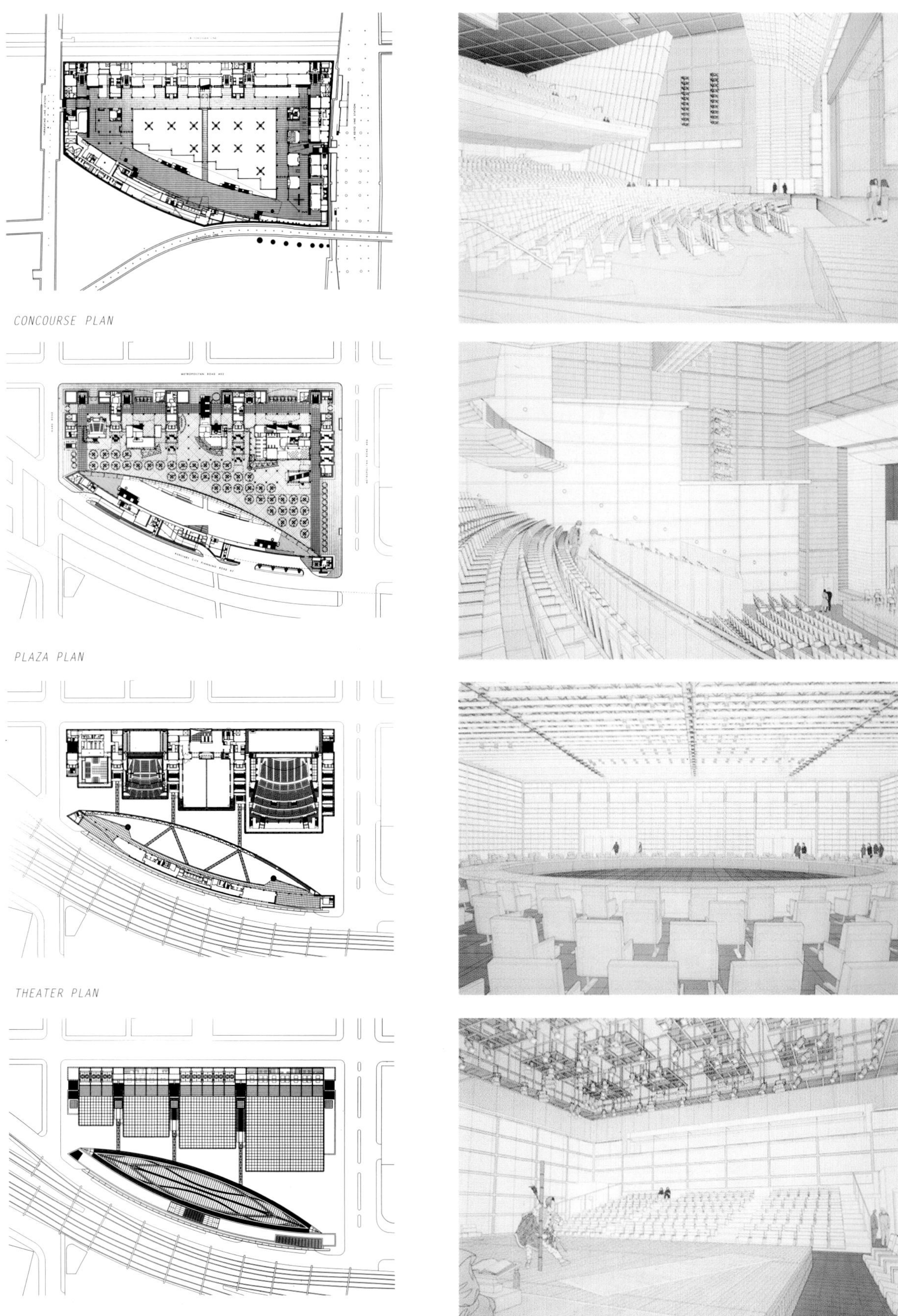

CONCOURSE PLAN

PLAZA PLAN

THEATER PLAN

ROOF PLAN

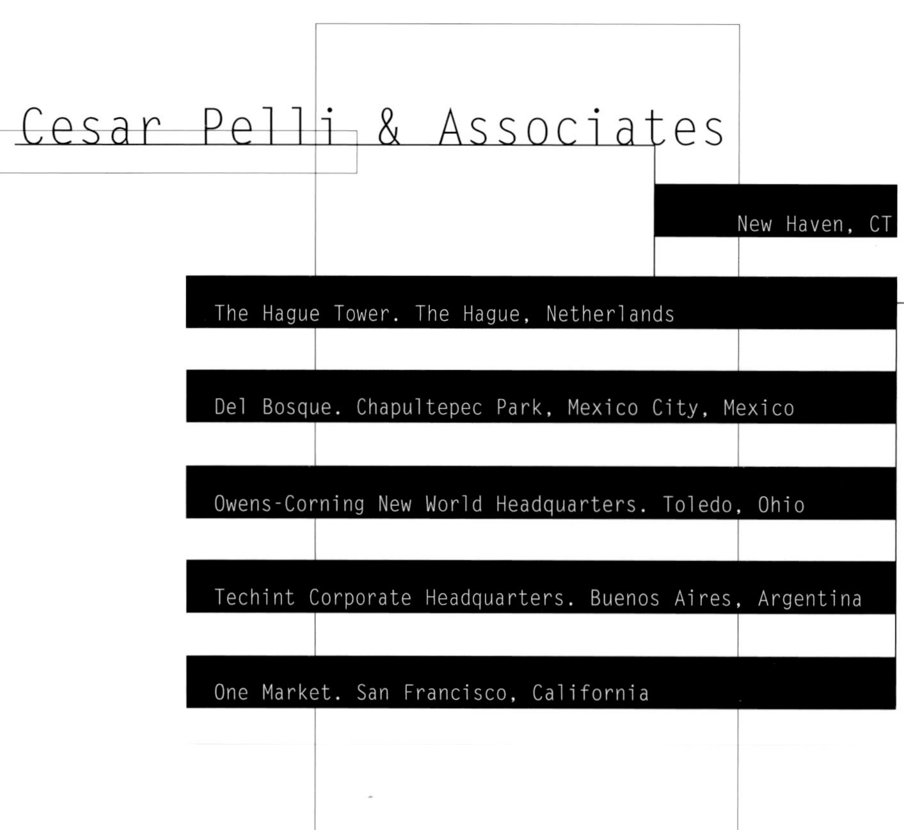

Cesar Pelli & Associates
New Haven, CT
The Hague Tower. The Hague, Netherlands
Del Bosque. Chapultepec Park, Mexico City, Mexico
Owens-Corning New World Headquarters. Toledo, Ohio
Techint Corporate Headquarters. Buenos Aires, Argentina
One Market. San Francisco, California

Cesar Pelli & Associates is a full-service architectural firm with substantial credentials and experience. The firm's first commission in 1977 was the Museum of Modern Art expansion and renovation in New York City. Subsequent projects have continued a consistent history of high quality built work of increasing variety. Clients, programs, sites, and budgets are diverse, enabling Cesar Pelli & Associates to gain expertise in a broad array of building types. The firm has worked with corporate, governmental and private clients to design office towers, laboratories, airports, museums, performing arts centers, mixed-use projects, and public spaces. The number of commissions the firm accepts is carefully limited to ensure a high degree of personal involvement by its principals.

The firm is structured to work in two modes: first, as a traditional full-service firm; second, as a specialized design firm capable of working in complex associations and collaborations. Successful association with other architects has made it possible to accept large-scale commissions while still remaining structured as an atelier, an atmosphere more typical of a much smaller firm. The firm has 75 full-time employees.

The Use of Computers at Cesar Pelli & Associates

The widespread use of personal computers in business and industry has provided architects with a variety of new tools. Cesar Pelli & Associates has maximized this technology to support many aspects of practice. Fifty different systems are used, including desktop units, high-powered CAD stations with high-resolution displays, and laptops for design, administration, and accounting. Of particular interest has been the evolution of the computer as a design tool in the studio. The design process is based on the generation of multiple options created and studied principally in three-dimensional models. The first PC-based drawing packages, which ran on state-of-the-art hardware at the time, were capable of only two-dimensional graphics that imitated manual drafting conventions. The firm's first use of computers was therefore limited to generating production documents, including detailed plans, elevations, sections, and pattern studies. But because the systems could not produce three-dimensional images with sufficient speed or quality, earlier implementations of CAD were peripheral to the design process in the studio. The firm's computer-aided design capabilities have evolved with innovations in software and hardware; it started with AutoCAD version 2.6 on the IBM-PC compatible 80286 system. Release 10, running on 80386 processors, was the first version to offer viable three-dimensional modeling capabilities

to the designers. It was initially used to study complex forms that were difficult to model in paper and cardboard. Multiple options of such forms can be quickly produced and edited before attempting more detailed physical models. The design of many projects has since been developed by simultaneously using both physical models and computer-generated models. Each technique informs the other throughout the design process. With the advent of AutoCAD 12 and the 486 processor, true three-dimensional modeling can be accomplished, compatible with the visually-oriented design process.

In one project, Cesar Pelli envisioned a series of architectural inserts to existing public spaces. These elements are a collection of complex aluminum frame pergolas, canopies, lighting structures, and pavilions with multiple intersections and connections. The design team simultaneously constructed computer and plastic models of these forms, using the computer to explore various configurations in detail, and only building plastic models of certain alternatives. The team then used the computer to document the technical details of the design for construction. Concurrently, the computer models were used by a professional renderer to create realistic three-dimensional drawings composited with digitized images of the existing space.

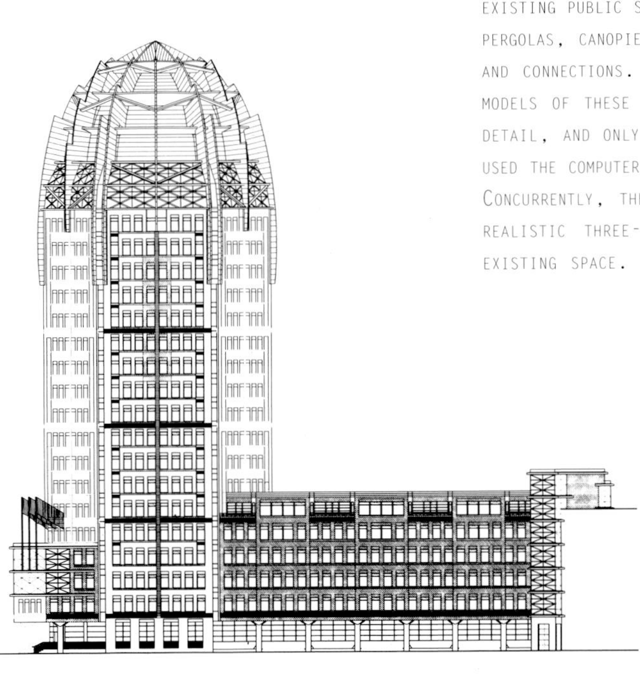

Today, computers are more fully integrated with the design process. In addition to the exploration of formal composition, new rendering software enables designers to see realistic representations of the design in relatively short time, directly in a CAD environment. Although super-realistic renderings are becoming popular, they are less useful to the design process at Cesar Pelli & Associates where there is a preference for a degree of abstraction to clarify formal relationships among architectural elements. However, computer-generated renderings have become important components of the firm's work to complement hand drawings and study models.

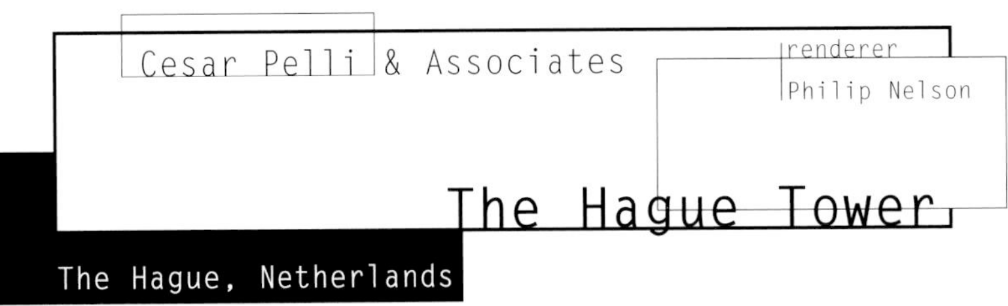

Cesar Pelli & Associates

renderer
Philip Nelson

The Hague Tower

The Hague, Netherlands

The hexagonal tower will be the corporate headquarters for an insurance company. The project is within the De Resident Master Plan designed by Robert Krier in cooperation with Sjoerd Soeters. The Master Plan intends to extend the old city fabric into an area of The Hague that was bombed during World War II.

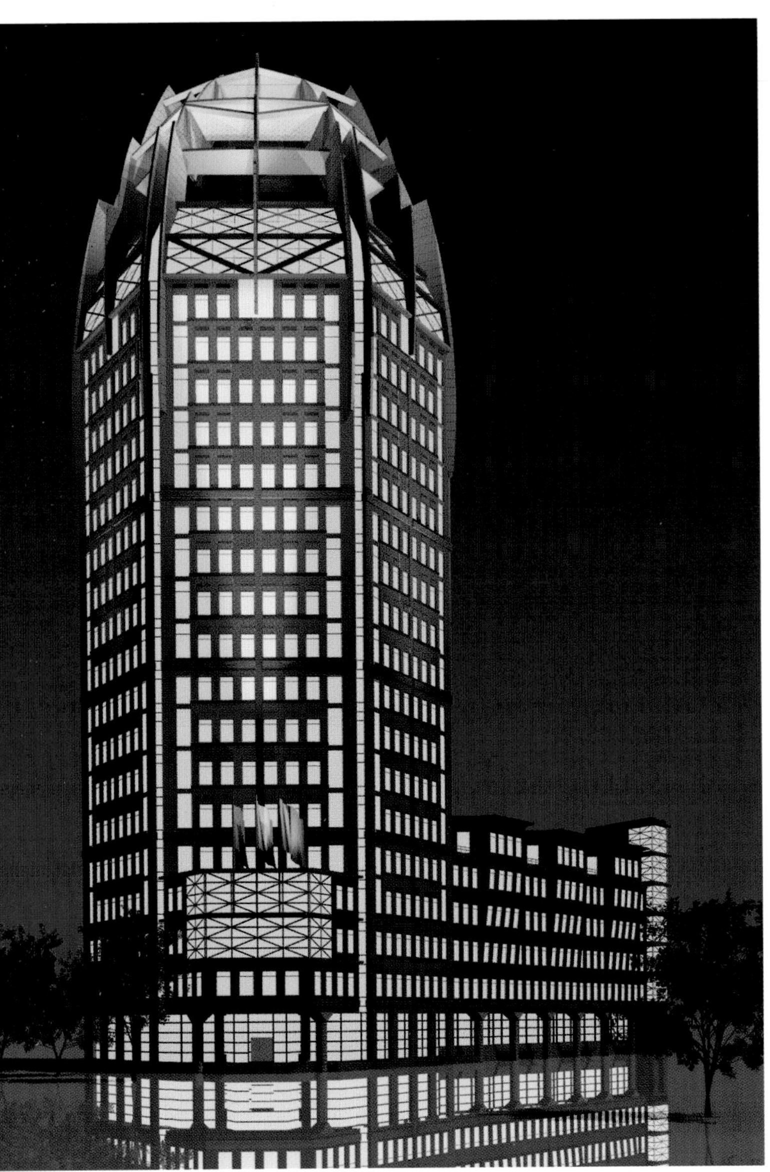

The 240,000-square-foot brick and ceramic-tile tower will rise 20 stories, with two levels of underground parking and below-grade functions, as well as a five-story wing. The fifth floor of the wing will have a corporate restaurant, meeting rooms, and a media center. A public gallery will be located on the ground floor of the tower, with a private garden court on the back of the building.

Acting as the visual terminus of the Boulevard Koningnne Gracht, and taking advantage of views to the adjacent Koekamp city park, the tower will terminate in a top constructed of colored-metal clad planes which define a dome. The facade will be patterned with five colors of brick and ceramic tile.

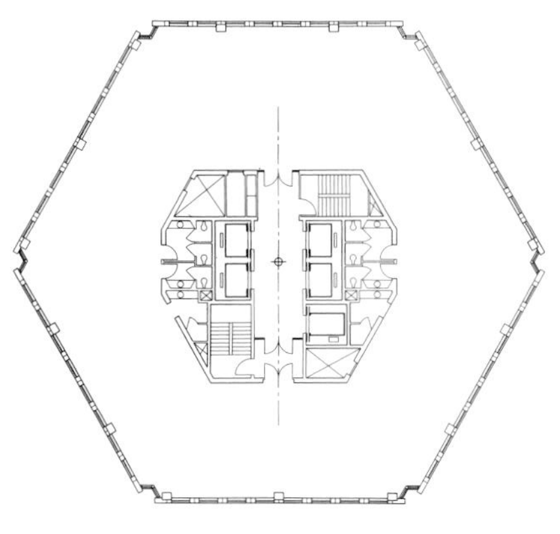

TYPICAL FLOOR PLAN

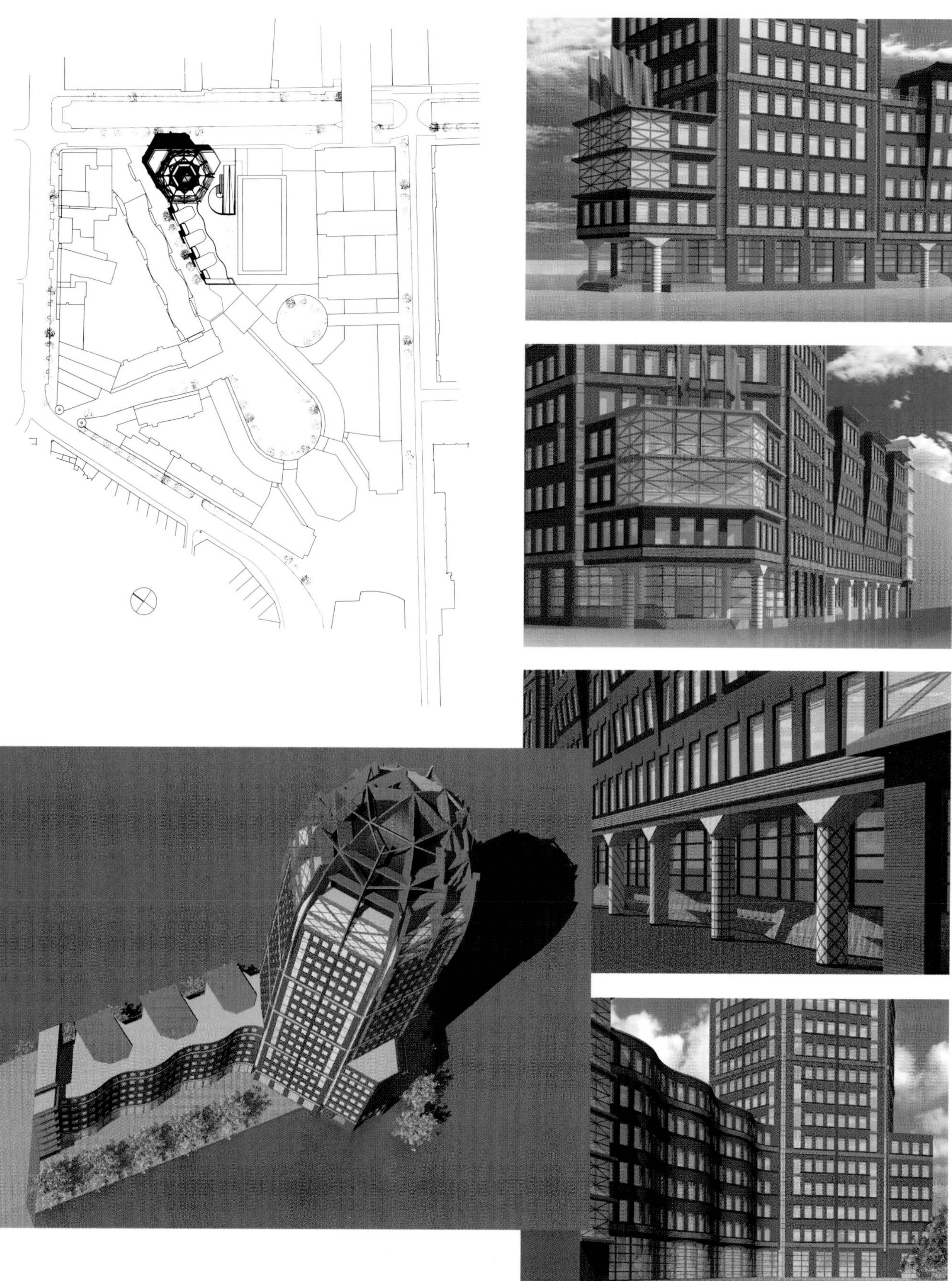

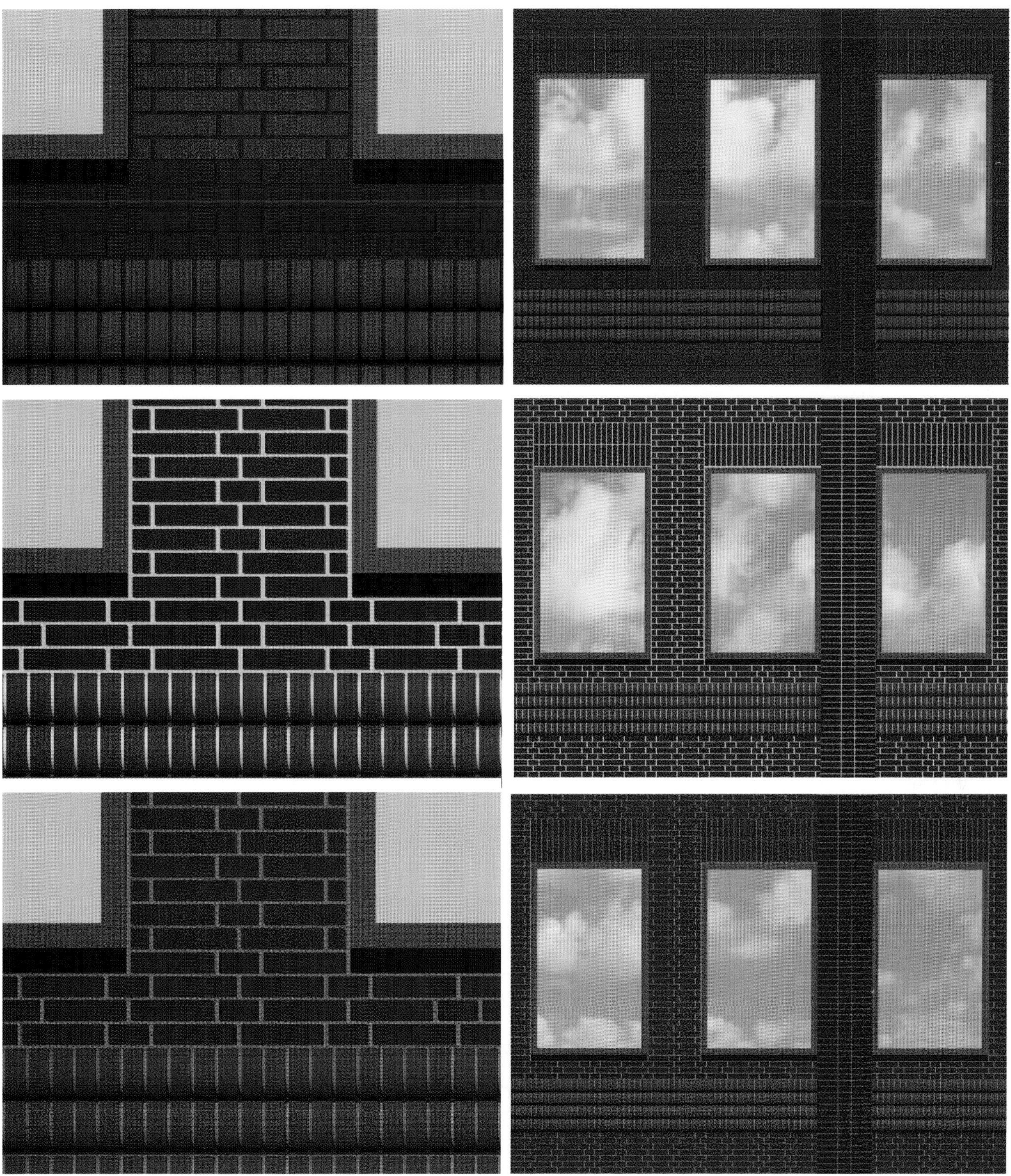

The influence of using alternative colors of mortar with the same brick pattern was studied to evaluate changes in the overall color palette of the building facade and the different impressions that each colorway presented. The bricks were drawn first and various color planes were added behind these elements to reveal each alternative.

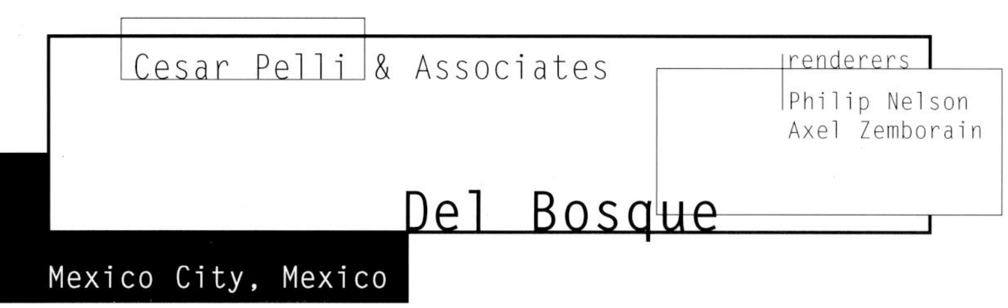

Cesar Pelli & Associates

renderers
Philip Nelson
Axel Zemborain

Del Bosque

Mexico City, Mexico

Del Bosque comprises one 13-story office building, two 31-story residential towers, a 5,000-square-foot health club, and a three-level below-ground parking facility. The four buildings are situated on a triangular piece of land in the Polanco District and have been designed with multi-curved planes that maximize the panoramic view of Chapultepec Park.

The office building has a curved triangular form that responds to the geometry of the site and marks the corner of the block. The building is clad in Brazilian green granite cast in precast spandrels, semireflective insulated glass, and painted-aluminum curtainwall. The precast/granite spandrels have recessed moldings to bring forward the glass wall, stressing the design idea of a taut skin.

The apartment buildings are twin towers designed as sculptural pylons with multiple curved planes, set-backs, and balconies to maximize views and enhance their residential quality. The buildings are clad in alternating bands of butt-glazed glass; red precast spandrels with red sandstone aggregate; and accents of glazed Mexican tiles.

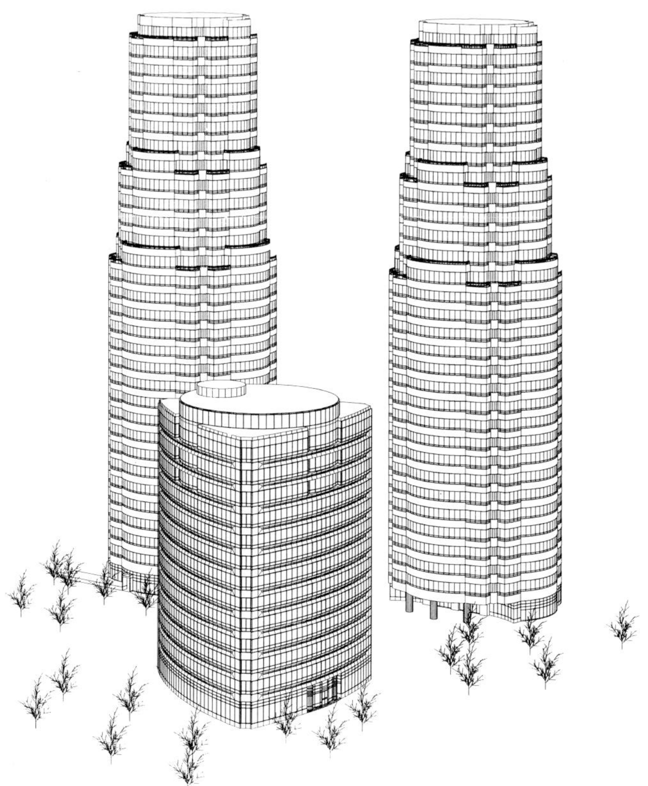

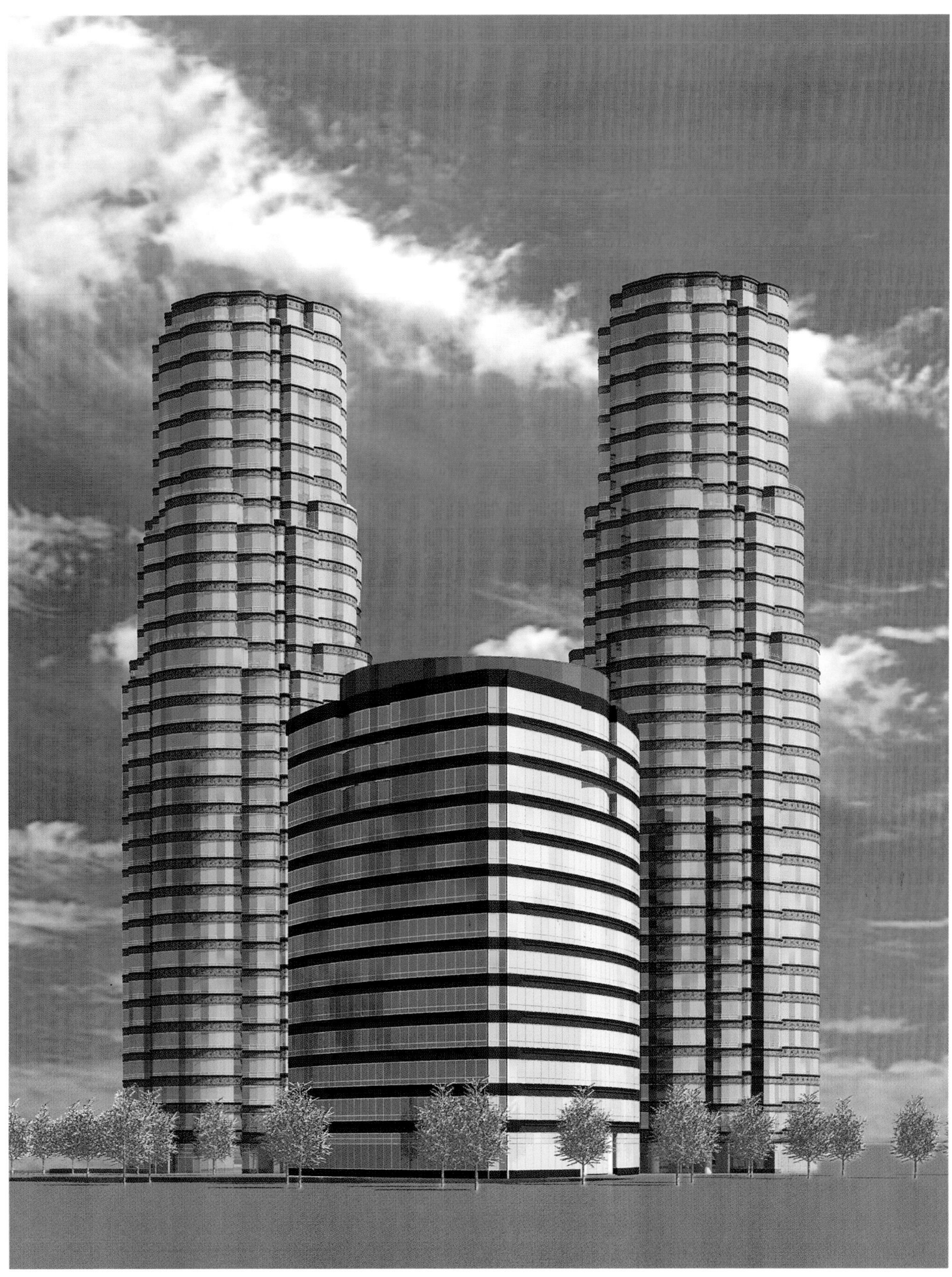

Cesar Pelli & Associates

renderers
Philip Nelson
Axel Zemborain

Owens-Corning New World Headquarters

Toledo, Ohio

The Owens-Corning world headquarters is located on a peninsula bounded by Swan Creek and the Maumee River directly adjacent to the heart of Toledo's business center. The 400,000-square-foot headquarters building will house 1,100 employees in a campus-like environment organized around a large central courtyard.

The unique location and configuration of the headquarters will provide a new focal point and landmark for Toledo. The building is an assemblage of component parts linked together by glass-enclosed connectors. The workplace component, which curves to provide extensive views of Toledo and the river, is clad in ceramic frit-patterned reflective glass on the river side, and clear glass on the courtyard side. In contrast, the ancillary components will be clad in various colors of glazed brick. The centrally-located lobby component is topped with a striking painted metal panel roof, penetrated with small clerestory windows. The roof form is inspired by the color and design of the Owens-Corning corporate logo. The change of material, color, and texture emphasizes the campus feel of the design.

The workplace component is an open-office environment that maximizes access to views and natural sunlight adjacent to a three-story glass atrium. The atrium and glass-clad stairways are designed to encourage interaction and "casual collision." The ancillary components house special-use functions such as dining, auditorium, training, and a wellness center. All the components have access to the central courtyard. The courtyard is designed to provide the widest range of uses, from symphony orchestra performances, to dining, to intimate business meetings.

The interior materials are modest but durable, reflecting the corporation's policy and image. The lobby will have a gray-green slate floor with back-lit cascading plaster walls topped with the roof form clad in bright red ceramic tile. The public areas have either terrazzo or carpet on the floor, with acoustic tile ceilings and gypsum board walls. Highlights of brick and wood will be used in special areas. The workplace and ancillary areas have carpet or rubber tile floors, acoustic tile ceilings, and gypsum board walls. The use of color is extensive. Also, glass artist Thomas Patti has created several large integrated art-glass panels that demonstrate Owens-Corning fiberglass technology, and are located throughout the headquarters.

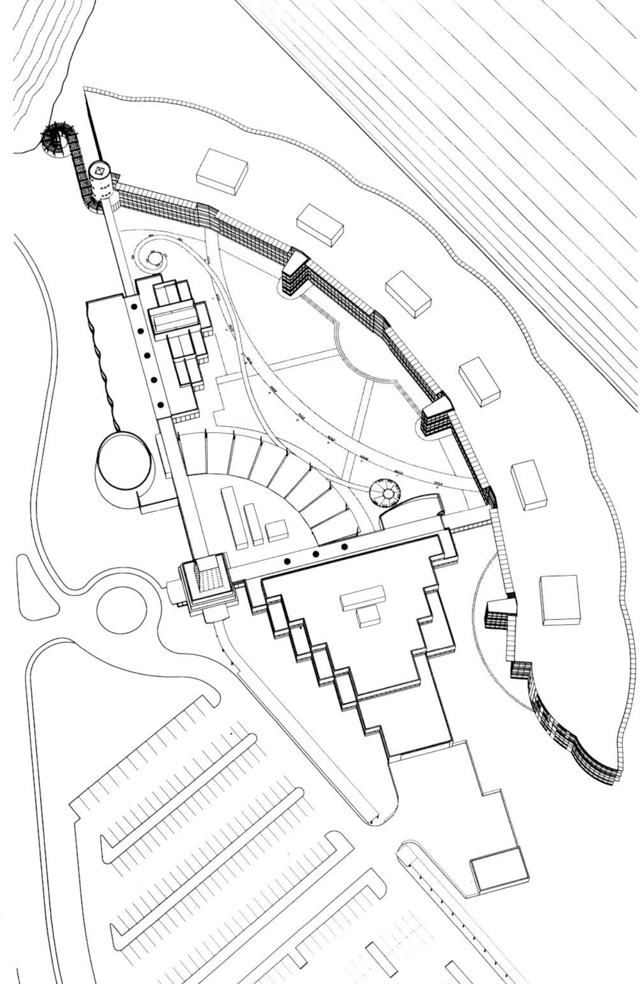

Cesar Pelli & Associates

renderer
Philip Nelson

Techint Corporate Headquarters

Buenos Aires, Argentina

The site for the Techint headquarters building is located in the central area of Buenos Aires, occupying half a block on Avenida Córdoba, Calle Reconquista, and Calle Viamonte. The building will have 630,000 square feet: 350,000 square feet in 15 floors above grade and 280,000 square feet in four floors below grade, including two garage levels.

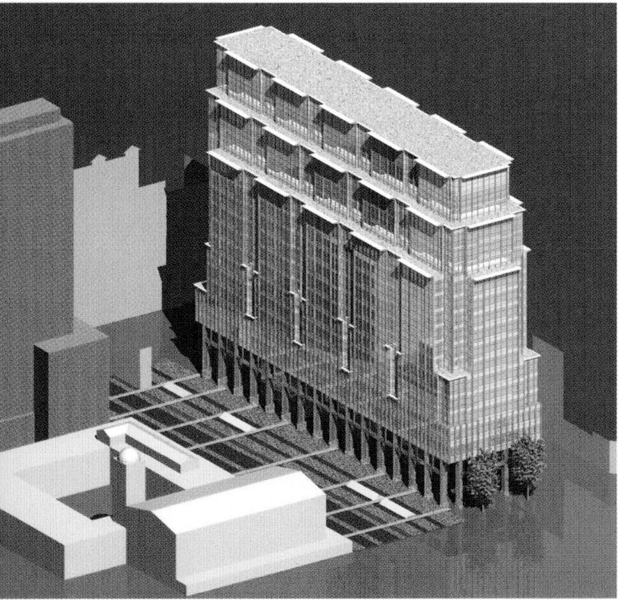

The project has to comply with strict limitations imposed by the urban planning norms for this particular site. These norms define not only the maximum building envelope but also its proportions, setbacks, and location. Furthermore, the norms decree an open ground-floor space 10 meters high to allow for views toward the Convent of Santa Catalina.

The building fronts Avenida Córdoba and defines an urban facade along Calle Reconquista. The plan proportions allow the creation of a public plaza that links the building of the central administration for the University of Buenos Aires with Avenida Córdoba, leaving open a wide perspective toward the historical monument of the Convent of Santa Catalina. The volume, large for the central area of Buenos Aires, is articulated with setbacks, recesses, and other modulations at several scales to make it a more sympathetic presence in the city.

The Techint headquarters is enclosed in a sophisticated silver metal and glass curtainwall. The building is elegant and memorable, with a character expressing efficiency and advanced technology. The silver is the predominant gray color of Buenos Aires, but is enriched with reflections and expresses a contemporary technology.

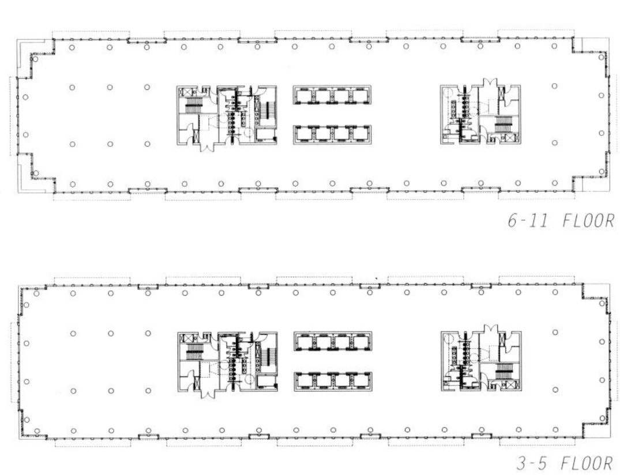

6-11 FLOOR

3-5 FLOOR

Cesar Pelli & Associates
renderers
Michael Sechman
Rob Narracci
One Market
San Francisco, California

One Market is a 1.5 million-square-foot multi-tenant office building complex, located in the San Francisco central business district. The project includes major renovation and improvement to two office towers of 42 stories and 27 stories, new ground-level public spaces, the design of retail facilities, and two levels of below-ground parking.

One Market transforms both the interior and exterior spaces, creating a new destination in San Francisco. Its design grows from a strong San Franciscan tradition of idiosyncratic structures full of optimism, charm, and friendly welcome. A six-story hexagonal gate tower of open lightweight steel marks the public space. A lacy pylon at the Mission Street entrance echoes the forms of the interior pavilion; this gate tower marks not only the entrance to One Market, but also the edge of the city toward the water. It was designed as a clear marker, visible from a distance on Mission Street and from adjacent, developing waterfront areas.

In addition to refurbishing exterior facades, ground floor public areas, and elevator lobbies, the renovation dramatically improves the aesthetic quality of all public spaces within the project boundaries and creates a truly memorable pedestrian space in San Francisco.

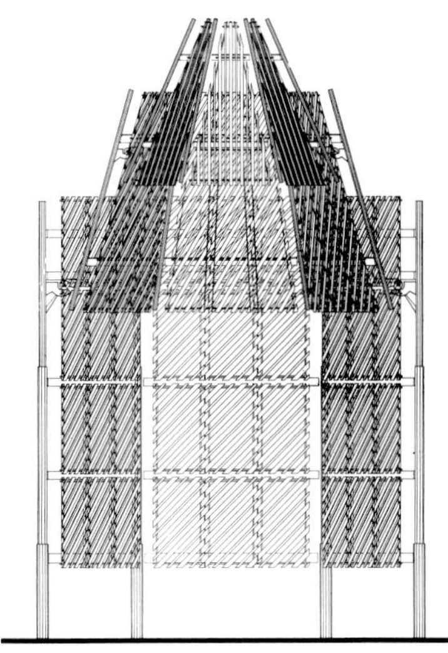

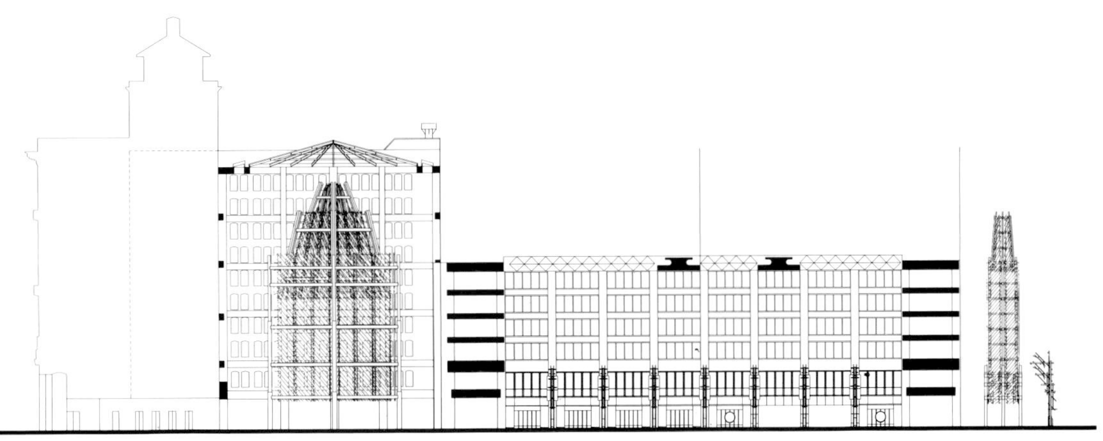

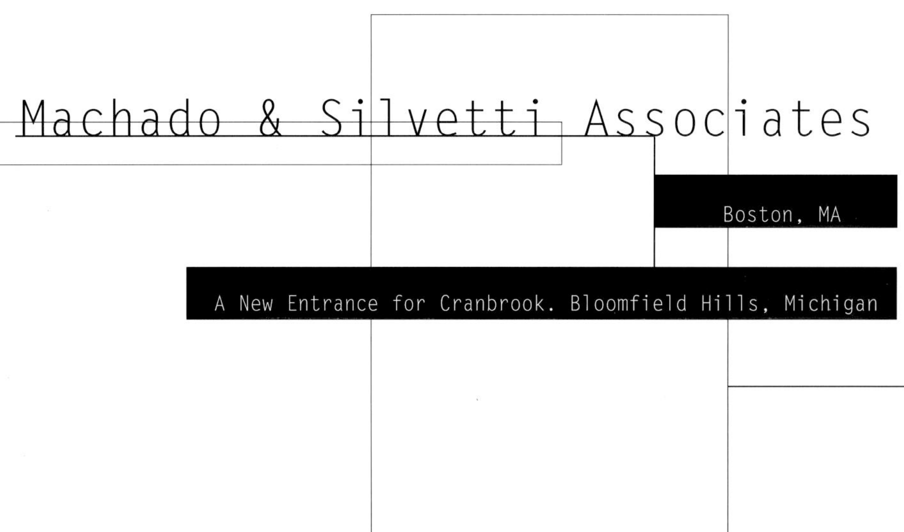

Machado & Silvetti Associates
Boston, MA
A New Entrance for Cranbrook. Bloomfield Hills, Michigan

Machado and Silvetti Associates Inc. is an internationally recognized planning and design firm known for distinctive urban spaces and unique works of architecture in the United States and abroad. The form and image of the design work comes from the particular client and project, and the specific needs and place for which a proposal is designed. The work does not espouse any single architectural style, but strives to find that which is unique and important within a given project, and to express that urbanistically and architecturally. The projects are distinctive for their conceptual clarity and visual intensity.

The Use of Computers at Machado & Silvetti Associates

The use of computers as an orthographic projection tool, such as in the modeling of a new entrance to the Cranbrook Academy, was especially potent. It allowed the accurate and efficient construction of difficult geometries (tapered brick coursings and angled limestone panels). Subtle perspectival phenomena could be studied and accurately fine-tuned. Furthermore, a deeper authenticity and resonance were achieved in the proposal by texture-mapping brick patterns created from scanned photos of existing patterns at Cranbrook.

In the development of these computer renderings, special attention was given to the rich tradition of hand-rendered perspectives in the office. On one level, materiality, light, shadow, and colors were carefully calculated, but a much deeper challenge was to create the unique narrative aspect the office has developed over time. Perspectives are often constructed as though the viewer were actively engaged in the unfolding architectural story. Just as a work of fiction may use the omniscient first person narrator to envelop the reader as a character, these sequences appear as stage sets carefully orchestrated through layering and framing.

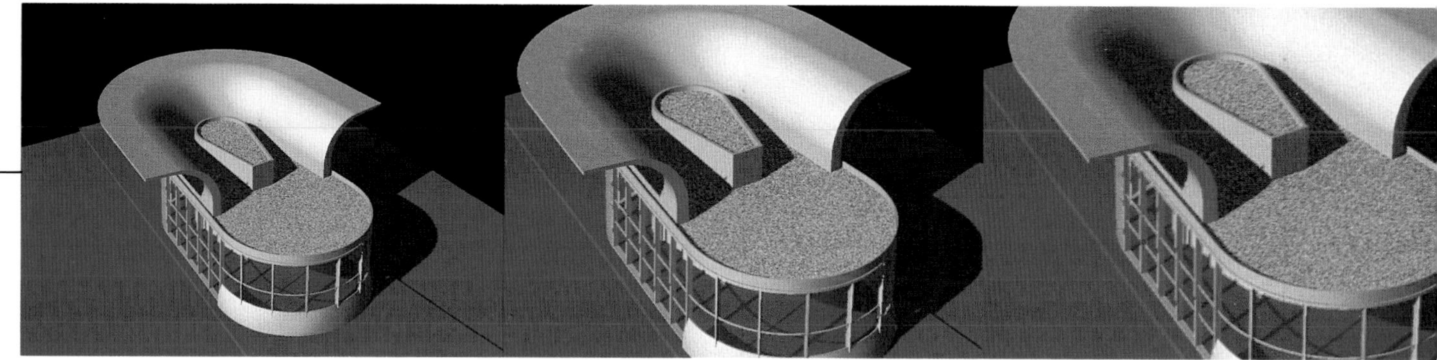

Machado and Silvetti Associates has always been integrally involved with the academic setting. This close association has allowed the utilization of advanced modeling techniques in the testing of ideas at an early stage. Now as a mature architectural firm with major commissions, a balance is more easily maintained between traditional and computer-aided design studies. There have been no lapses into technological solipsism at the expense of true architectural investigations. The study of unprecedented forms and the nuances in choreographed animation sequences has allowed not only a balance but a means of retaining a highly critical and efficient practice.

Machado & Silvetti Associates

renderer
Stephen Atkinson

A New Entrance for Cranbrook

Bloomfield Hills, Michigan

For this proposal, we understand an entrance to be no more than an opening in a vertical plane; a cut in a wall. Our wall occupies a diagonal line traced across the recommended building site (a rectangle with its eastern side parallel to, and 250 feet away from, Woodward Avenue; its northern and southern sides located 60 feet away from the property lines; and its western side limited by the recommended site boundary). This oblique, which cuts across the access and exit road, is a response to the asymmetrical approach (produced by the intensity of traffic arriving from the south). Hence the diagonal placement, which refers to a certain spirit of modernity and, in a way, to the inventive and critical nature of Cranbrook.

In this manner, the largest possible wall is generated. It is also the highest wall on campus: 30 feet tall at its peak. This ambitious and resolute size is a response to two different conditions: the vastness of the landscape around it (as well as the size of the campus to which it gives access on Woodward Avenue) and the equally vast and resolute cultural role played by Cranbrook as an art institution.

The wall is made out of a steel tube structure which carries steel-framed brick panels on the outer front and is braced with concrete blocks, "buttresses" (limestone veneered), on the inner front. More importantly, when both brick and limestone "applications" stop, the steel tube structure is clad in steel sheets producing the effect of a six-inch-wide free-standing steel wall.

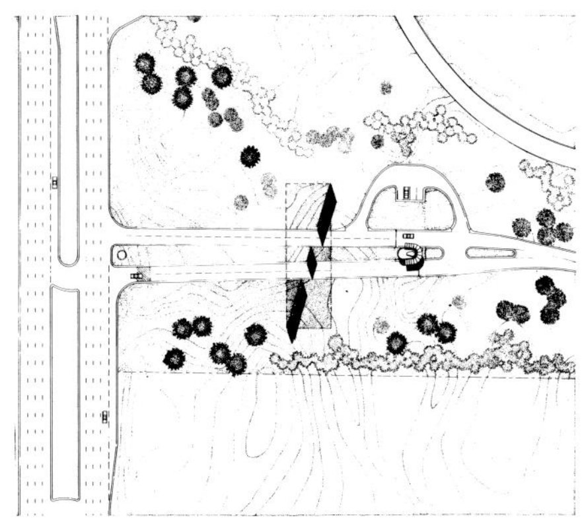

The brick panels are made of diverse brick patterns displayed against a common background on which variations are played. Motifs, inventions, and direct references to Saarine and found conditions abound and coexist with authorial quotations. The security booth is an altogether separate and distinct building which must not detract from the wall's uniqueness. It is located well into the site and directly related to the parking area on the exit road side. It is a technically-minded and fully pragmatic little building.

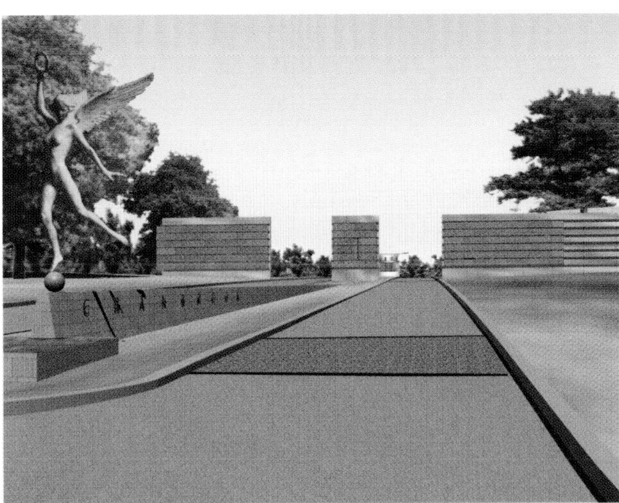

These images comprise the main entry and exit sequences through the proposal. They were modeled in Computer Vision and rendered using a Silicon Graphics workstation. Scanned images used in the renderings include an early 20th century sculpture, trees and bricks from the Cranbrook campus (arranged into patterns using Artisan).

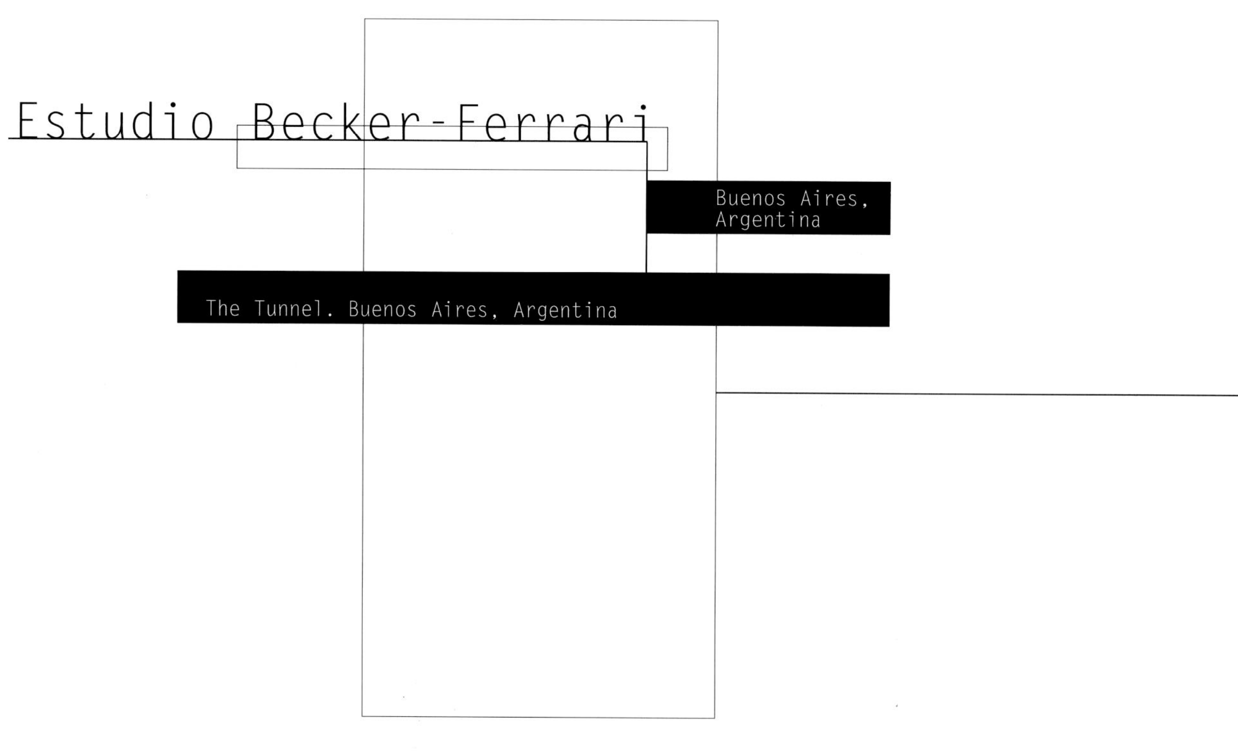

Estudio Becker-Ferrari

Buenos Aires, Argentina

The Tunnel. Buenos Aires, Argentina

Estudio Becker-Ferrari is a new office headquartered in Buenos Aires, Argentina. Its principal partners, Alejandro Daniel Becker and Claudio Ferrari, have worked together on a variety of design projects, from interior design and small-scale architectural projects to urban design.

The Use of Computers at Estudio Becker-Ferrari

Hyper-reality's connotation is that of something beyond reality. Although a computer drawing cannot be the represented reality in itself, it embodies the double condition of being a representation of reality while being a reality in itself. Within this framework, computer drawings that represent architectural reality should be understood as the result of a sophisticated tool of design. This process enables the production of architecture and its study through computer drawings in order to depict a more acute representation of a future reality and makes possible a deeper research in architectural projects. It is through this notion of the use of computers as a more precise medium of representation, that they become a useful tool of design in architectural practice.

Becker-Ferrari's approach to computers is varied. In some cases they are used as sketching tools, in others as developmental instruments to be used in construction drawings, and in others to study materials and light effects. For the project presented here, AutoCAD and Accurender were indispensable tools for the design of the roofs' shapes. Not only did they enable the modeling of a complex double-curved form, but also allowed immediate changes to be made with great speed and precision. The computer also helped us to determine the shape, size, and precise location of each structural component of the roofs. At the same time, it became a research tool to further manipulate light effects, both natural and artificial. These fundamental issues in the design of the tunnel determined the specific use of computer drawings in the project's design development

Computers have also proved to be an effective tool of persuasion when the moment to present the project to a client arrives. Unlike traditional architectural drawings, computer drawings and their animation are easily understood by a lay audience, a fact that should not be overlooked.

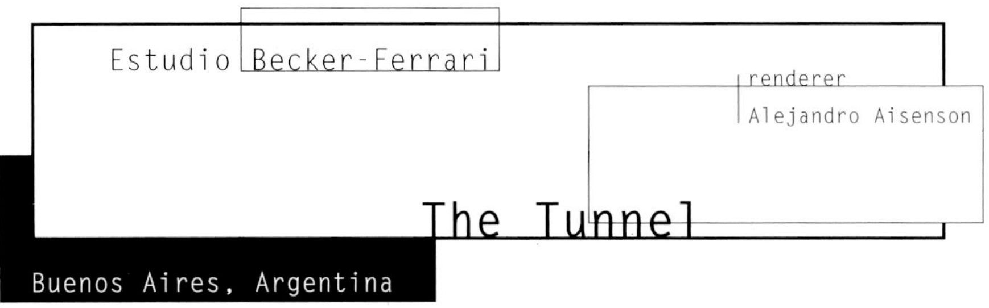

Estudio Becker-Ferrari
renderer
Alejandro Aisenson
The Tunnel
Buenos Aires, Argentina

The pedestrian tunnel (currently flooded), is situated on the corner of the avenues del Libertador and Sarmiento, framing the Spaniards Monument. It is in direct relation with the Zoo entrance and, most importantly, its location is near the center of the newly created nightlife area of Buenos Aires. It is also close to the Paseo Alcorta Shopping Mall and Plaza Italia.

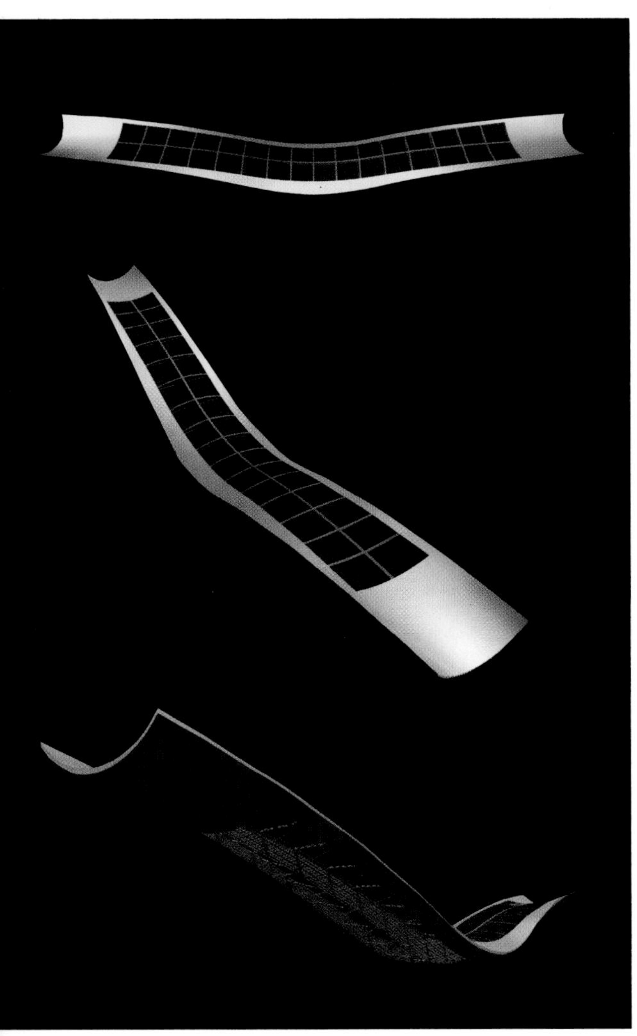

The main idea of the design is not only to recover the tunnel for its original use while keeping its original external characteristics, but also to create a new aesthetic in the interior according to its new use. The most innovative aspect of the project is that it will be used as a pedestrian tunnel during the day, and also as a gathering space for exhibitions, fashion shows, promotions, and nightlife.

The stairs at each end of the tunnel will be covered with a light, double-curved roof. This enables it to maintain its original characteristics and create a new scale for the entrance. At the same time, the two roofs give a better frame to the Spaniards Monument, reinforcing its character of landmark within the area. The roofs also have a very pragmatic function in preventing the entrance of water and allowing the artificial climatization of the interior.

The interior walls of the tunnel are clad with wood panels, and contain large-scale advertising signs. They also create the effect of a diverse and exciting urban life, therefore fulfilling the desire of the client. The two existing "heads" of the tunnel will be occupied by commercial spaces, mechanical and storage spaces, and a kitchen.

The night bar counters are movable and can be stored when not in use. This enables pedestrian use of the tunnel during the day.

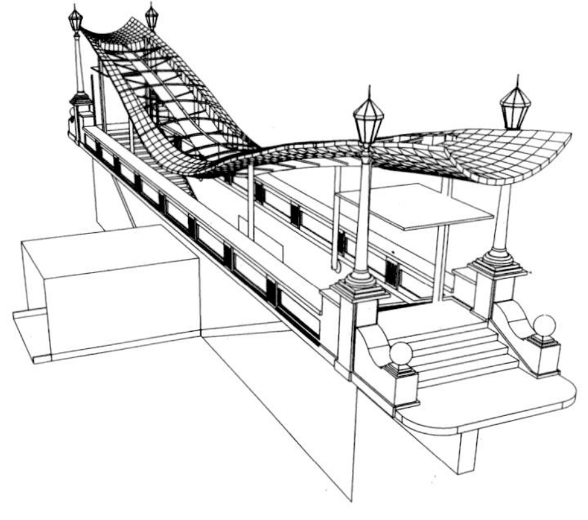

Coca-Cola

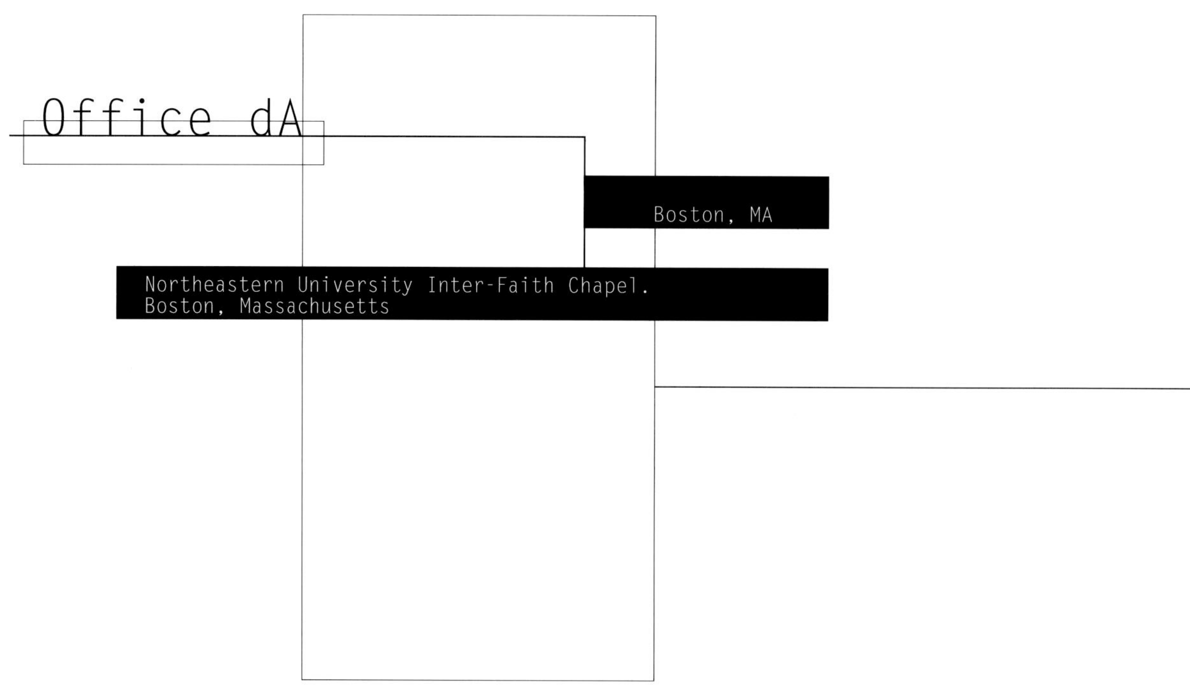

Office dA
Boston, MA
Northeastern University Inter-Faith Chapel.
Boston, Massachusetts

Office dA – Office of design and Architecture – is a young Boston-based firm that was established in 1986. Its principal partners include Rodolphe el Khoury, Monica Ponce de Leon, and Nader Tehrani. The work of Office dA is diverse in scope and scale, ranging from the design of interiors to the broader scale of urban design and infrastructure. Among other projects, various notable designs include: Miami-Public Infrastructure for the Tropics, a project that received first prize in the Boston Society of Architects Unbuilt Architecture Competition and is being published in *The New City Journal of Architecture* printed by Princeton Architectural Press; the Mill Road House, a design for a speculative house in Alabama, won an award in the 42nd Progressive Architecture Awards Program; the Greene House was published in the Spanish magazine *Casas Internacional* and the book *The New American House* by The Whitney Library of Design; the Northeastern University Inter-Faith Chapel, consisting of the redesign of a religious interior, is the subject of this publication.

The Use of Computers at Office dA

The use of computers in architectural firms, as in other practices, is by now commonplace. Among other areas, it has proven itself an indispensable tool for representation as well as production. Part of its prominence is due to its ability to create the "reality" effect in such a convincing and seamless manner. At the same time, given the nature of representation (and its diversity), the computer cannot produce all desired "realities"; the medium, as in most other cases, sets the limits of its representations.

At Office dA a variety of media is used, and the decision to work in a particular medium is made on a project-by-project basis to maximize the rhetorical charge of each design – to depict with precision the different realities of each project.

For the Northeastern University Inter-Faith Chapel, the computer was used for three general purposes: first, for the construction of complex geometries; second, for the easy duplication of repetitive modules; and third, for the rendering and design of specific lighting effects, all of which play a central role in this particular design.

The "draped" domes - figuratively hung ceilings - were a central feature of the design of the space: spherical surfaces, cut at the edges to produce a square figure in plan, articulated each with an oculus emanating beams of light onto three zones of the space. Given the complexity of their geometry, the computer gave obvious advantages, not only in drawing them with precision, but also enabling their subsequent viewing from multiple vantage points.

The curtainwalls, on the other hand, were geometrically rectilinear and simple to draw. They included three different bay types that were distributed according to various functional criteria throughout the space. The computer thus enabled their repetition and distribution throughout the space with a certain ease, albeit to produce a non-repetitive and sporadic effect.

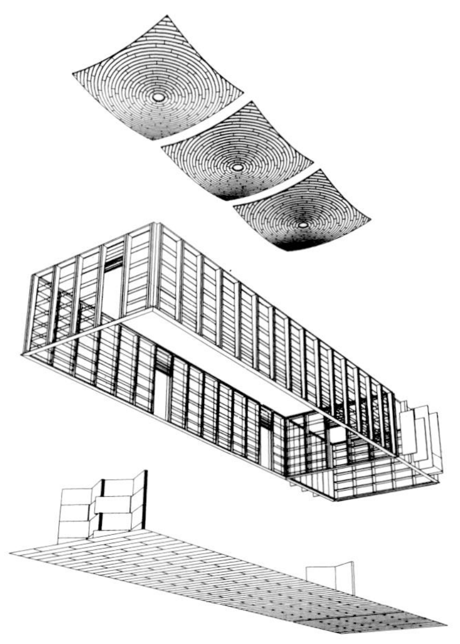

Most importantly, however, the computer was used in great part as a "sketching" tool, a process that is usually associated with hand drawings and pencil renderings. The virtue of the pencil sketch over the "photo-realist" representation has been its ability to fulfill certain rhetorical impulses - abstractions, exaggerations, deletions - with great speed as well as a certain precision. On the other hand, the computer has proved itself a malleable medium for rendering, once the general input of the project data has been completed. In this instance, we found the rendering of light - its reflections, its depths, and its ambiance - was "sketched" with much greater ease, speed, and sophistication through the computer.

Paradoxically, the realism of the materials in some of the images seems to detract from the conceptual focus of the project. The over-articulation of wood, of glass, and of metal supplanted the "ambiance of spirituality" produced by effects of light alone. As such, some of the black-and-white studies were generated to focus more directly on the light as a phenomenon itself - in essence, abstracting an element of "reality" allowed us to focus on the privileged rhetorical basis of the project.

Office dA

renderer
Ben Karty

Northeastern University Inter-Faith Chapel

Boston, Massachusetts

This project was commissioned by the Northeastern University Spiritual Life Center for the renovation and rehabilitation of the University's Inter-Faith Chapel - currently located on the second floor of the Ell Center in the heart of the campus.

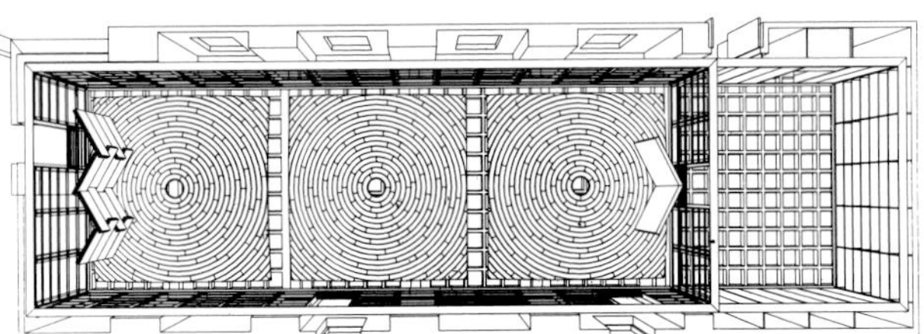

The space of the chapel is divided into two areas. A smaller room serves as a meeting room and library for books of the various faiths; it also holds the accessories needed in the rituals of various religions. The secular character of the room allows the juxtaposition of such icons without contradiction, as in a museum. A larger room with no specific religious iconography is to be used as a "sacred" space for prayer; this room is conceived as a luminous space. The diaphanous lighting - a rhetorical feature of many religious buildings - is contrary to one's expectations in this location, at the core of the building, and should clearly differentiate the chapel from other adjacent secular spaces.

The floor is refinished in large sheets of wood thin-ply, creating a monumental scale for a surface on which to pray - as used for Islamic as well as other religious rites. It is polished enough to acquire a reflective quality, consistent with the other elements of the space.

The walls are lined with a layered glass curtainwall (frosted or sandblasted) supported by wood columns and lit from behind. The cladding alters from bay to bay depending on the irregularities of the existing wall behind. Three variations are possible: where the existing wall is in close proximity, the glass curtainwall "drapes" to the ground, concealing the pilaster behind. Where there are niches, the glass hangs above the floor, high enough to allow access to the spotlights. The curtainwall is fully drawn in front of the entryways.

The ceiling embraces the pragmatic exigencies of the room (HVAC) and capitalizes on the modest proportions of the space to create visual drama from spatial tension. This unorthodox "hung-ceiling" is composed of hanging domes that drape down in glistening metal rings, heavy with suspended mass, light with reflected luminescence.

Skidmore, Owings & Merrill
Offices Worldwide
Logan International Airport. Boston, Massachusetts
Dulles International Airport Main Terminal Expansion. Chantilly, Virginia
San Francisco International Airport. Modernization Program San Francisco, California
101 Second Street. San Francisco, California
Swiss Bank Corporation. Stamford, Connecticut
Aramco. Dhahran, Saudi Arabia
Broadgate Development. London, England
World Trade Center. Berlin, Germany
Jin Mao Building. Shanghai, China

The Use of Computers at Skidmore, Owings & Merrill

Founded in 1936, Skidmore, Owings & Merrill is one of the leading architectural firms in the United States. The firm's sophistication in building technology applications and commitment to design quality have resulted in a portfolio that features some of the most important architectural accomplishments of this century. Today, with offices worldwide, SOM has completed more than 6,000 architecture, interior architecture, and planning projects located in more than 50 countries around the world. In the past several decades, the firm has been recognized internationally for the quality of its architectural design and production.

SOM uses a software system called Architecture and Engineering Series (AES) which is among the most advanced and flexible computer-aided design and drafting (CADD) systems available and is marketed in a joint venture with IBM. By integrating AES with other popular software, SOM is able to effectively use the computer in all aspects of the design process. Customized software that meets a client's individual and specific needs has also been developed.

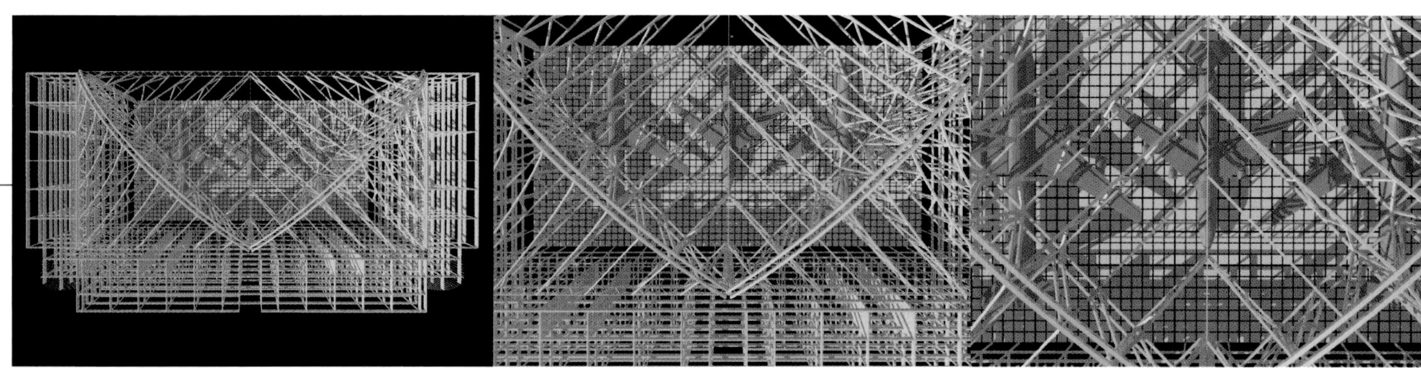

Computers are used by all disciplines in all phases of projects at SOM. Applications include three-dimensional modeling and rendering, urban planning, zoning analysis, project management, space programming, interior architecture, cost estimating, and complete construction documents. Structural and civil engineering modules are used for the design and analysis of structural systems, foundation mats, site work, and grading. Modules used by building services engineers perform energy analysis, HVAC load calculations, mechanical equipment selection, duct sizing, and lighting design. Interior design applications facilitate programming, blocking and stacking, furniture ordering and inventory, and facilities management.

SOM's use of CADD is a key component of the quality control program. While most CADD systems are primarily drawing oriented, emulating the drafting process, SOM's application of CADD facilitates methods which are building oriented - in that it creates an integrated database defining the project in all respects - from which both drawings and various types of reports are produced. This approach provides far greater benefits in terms of accuracy, coordination, and completeness of the design. It also permits the exploration of a greater number of design alternatives.

One of the most exciting aspects of SOM computer system is its comprehensive ability to generate three-dimensional representations of the design and its evolution in the design process. These images and procedures, literally bring the building to life at a very early stage in its development. The system provides dynamic graphics that are highly successful in presenting the project and providing potential tenants with a vision of the design.

Above: *KAL Operation Center, Kimpo International Airport. Seoul, Korea.*
Right: *Hong Kong Convention Centre. Hong Kong.*

Skidmore, Owings & Merrill

renderers
Scott Harrison
Marinha Mascheroni
Ken Lewis
Yangwei Yee
Don Fedorko

Logan International Airport Modernization Program

Boston, Massachusetts

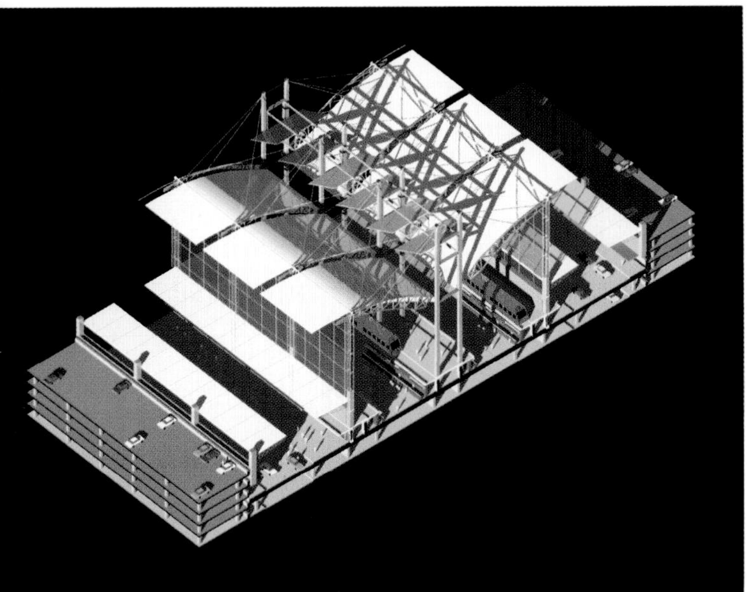

This project was won in a limited competition. In a parallel effort with the concept planning phase for the billion-square-foot expansion of the airport, the program establishes thorough design guidelines, and sets the architectural imagery and vocabulary for the airport.

Airport components detailed in the design guidelines include a new Terminal A, the expansion of the existing Terminal E, a parking garage, a hotel, a people-mover system, airport roadways, and a complete landscape program. The guidelines identify design elements that range from the forms of interior and exterior architectural expression, to the relationships between new and existing facilities, to types and quality of finishes and the selection of materials and colors.

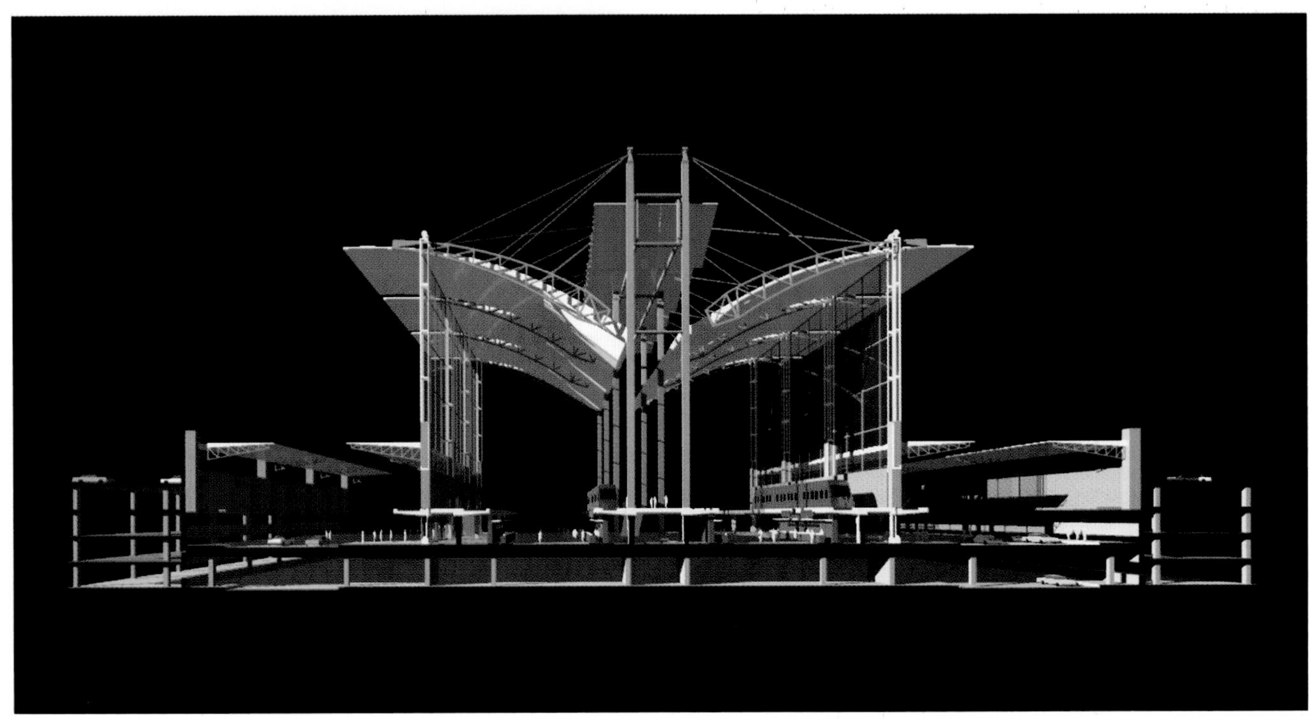

Skidmore, Owings & Merrill

renderers Scott Harrison
David Martin

Dulles International Airport Main Terminal Expansion

Chantilly, Virginia

The earliest realization of the concept of the separation of landside and airside components, Dulles Airport, designed by Eero Saarinen, became an architectural and functional model for much subsequent airport design after its completion in 1962.

The current expansion of the landmark Main Terminal building increases the annual passenger handling capacity from 12 million to 50 million passengers per year. The catenary roof structure, concrete podium, and glass curtain-wall is replicated to the east and west, housing ticketing, check-in, baggage claim, and support functions. The expansion of below-ground facilities for baggage handling, security, and passenger transport to airside under the apron minimizes visual impact, as well as disruption of aircraft circulation. The more than a million-square-foot project also includes demolition and reconstruction of enplanement and deplanement ramps and overall renovation of the existing terminal. SOM also conducted the expansion master plan review, designed the prototype for the midfield concourse buildings, and designed the 1991 International Arrivals Building.

FROM GATE

Skidmore, Owings & Merrill

renderers Peter Little
Leo Chow

San Francisco International Airport Modernization Program

San Francisco, California

The $275 million, seven-level International Terminal building is the centerpiece and the largest component of San Francisco International Airport's expansion plan. The new $2.4 billion development program is intended to accommodate current and future passenger needs and maintain SFO as the premier gateway to the Pacific. The 1.6 million-square-foot International Terminal complex will increase services to accommodate 16 new international gates for a total of 26 international gates, and 12 new gates in addition to the eight for the

latest generation aircraft. The terminal, which currently processes 1,200 passengers per hour, will be capable of processing 5,000 arriving passengers per hour. Processing time will decrease from nearly two hours to just 45 minutes. In addition, there will be 140,000 square feet of space for revenue-generating concessions, including duty-free shops, restaurants, and airline lounges. The building also houses the airport's administrative offices.

The wing-like roof over the Departure Hall is the principal feature of the design. The roof is a double cantilever that follows the moment diagram of the structure. Daylight gives it a floating quality, while the clear and patterned glass of the curtainwall at the entrance gives the interior a transparent and luminous quality.

The joint venture of SOM, Del Campo & Maru, and Michael Willis & Associates was selected for the project after winning an invited design competition sponsored by the airport.

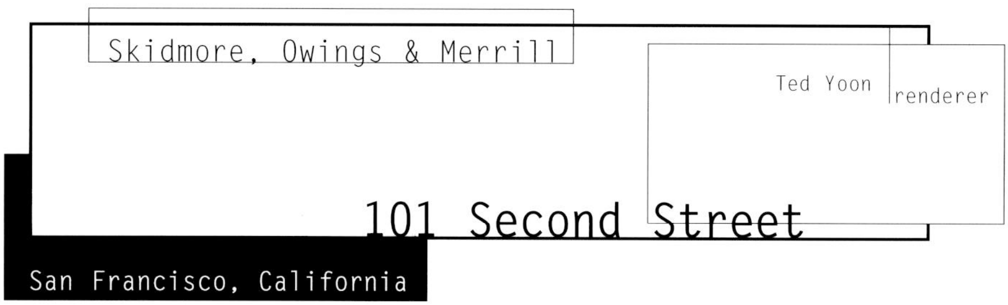

Skidmore, Owings & Merrill
Ted Yoon
renderer
101 Second Street
San Francisco, California

This investment office building is in San Francisco's downtown financial district. The 25-story, 409,000-square-foot building is set back from the corner of Mission and Second streets, with an enclosed terrace anchoring the corner. Its greenhouse enclosure is designed to match the cornice line of an historic building next door.

A landscaped setting that incorporates works of art as a visual feature provides weatherproof outdoor space adjoining the 20,650 square feet of retail space at street level. Another public amenity is a rooftop sculpture garden that overlooks the City's South of Market (SoMa) district. Designed to give skyline identity to a major tenant while fitting compatibly into the immediate context, the building's light-toned granite-and-glass facade is modernist in spirit, relating visually to such landmark buildings as SOM's One Bush Street, the former Crown Zellerbach Headquarters, and Timothy Pflueger's Pacific Tower.

Skidmore, Owings & Merrill

renderer Maria Alataris

Swiss Bank Corporation

Stamford, Connecticut

The new Swiss Bank Corporation complex is a distinguished group of buildings that will serve as a southern gateway to the city. The 12-acre campus, to be developed in three phases, will provide 1.4 million square feet of occupiable space, including offices and trading areas, parking facilities, and outdoor amenities for private use and use by the public. Along Washington Boulevard, the new complex is set back in a large outdoor park which is the major entrance to the project and is also an amenity for the public, to be enjoyed by city residents as well as employees of the company.

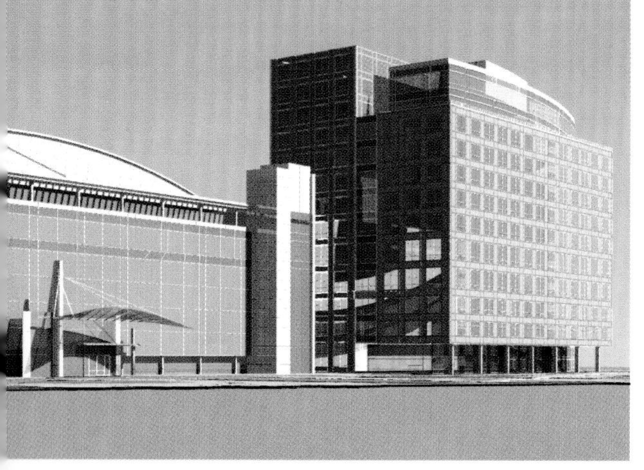

A 12-story office building and an adjacent seven-story trading pavilion to accommodate 2,000 employees will comprise the first phase of the project. Along with the office building, this phase will provide 1,400 parking spaces in four levels above grade and one level below grade for a total of 367,000 square feet. The core of the complex is a fifth-level lobby elevated above the parking areas, retail, health club, and support functions on the lower floors.

A 20-story, 500,000-square-foot office building located to the east of the first-phase buildings will be a future phase of the project. This phase entails the horizontal expansion of the trading floor which will add two bays, 300 trading positions, and corresponding support spaces. It will also incorporate 390,000 square feet of parking. The last phase of the project will be a 16-story, 350,000-square-foot office building and 350,000 square feet of structured parking. A two-story bridge will link the last phase to the sky-lobby level of the other buildings in the complex.

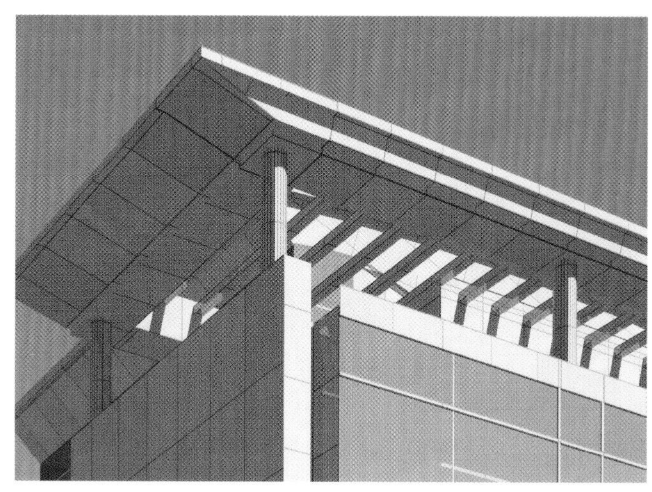

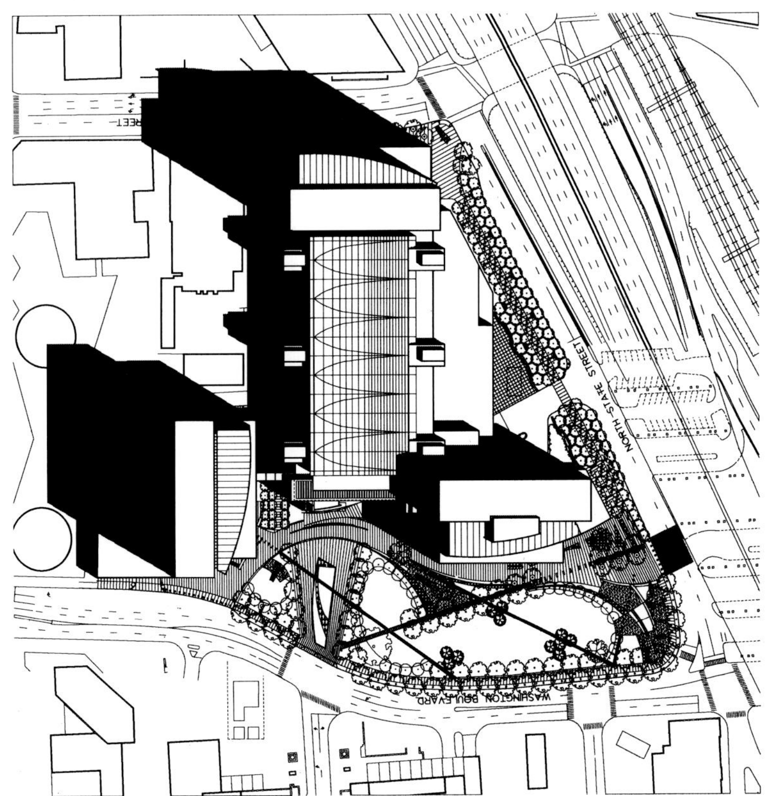
NORTH STATE STREET
WASHINGTON BOULEVARD

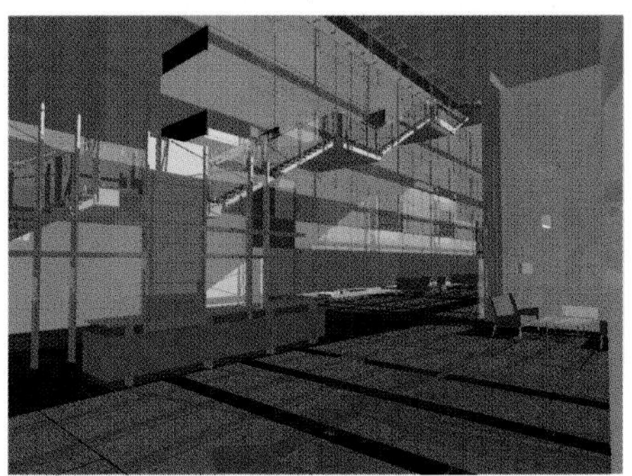

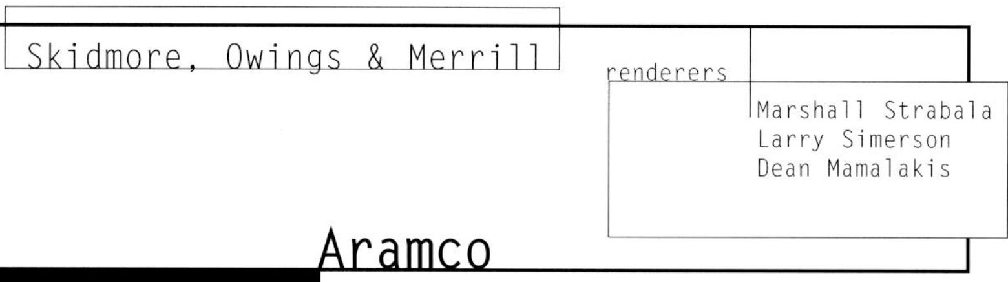

Skidmore, Owings & Merrill

renderers

Marshall Strabala
Larry Simerson
Dean Mamalakis

Aramco

Dhahran, Saudi Arabia

The 350,000-square-foot complex is planned in three phases to incorporate new office and mixed-use buildings within an existing campus of technical, research, and administrative buildings. The focal point of the complex is a new 20-story corporate headquarters tower consisting of two curvilinear pieces, 10 and 20 stories high, that enclose a 10-story central atrium.

The tower's exterior is a collection of expressed components, materials, and shapes. The harsh desert sun is controlled by brises-soleils of vertical glass fins, stainless-steel trusses, and horizontal sun shades. The broad eastern facade is broken by a set of stacked, three-story atria set against a 12-story black granite shear wall that ties the curving forms to the rectilinear geometry of the existing buildings. A covered two-story galleria terminates in the atrium of the new corporate building and features a 200-meter-long exhibition wall.

Skidmore, Owings & Merrill

Broadgate Development

London, England

renderers
Nate Kaiser
Michel Mossessian
Walt Bransford
Michael Gaffney
Pete Bochek

The master plan, architectural, and structural engineering design of 10 buildings in the Broadgate complex is part of the largest single development in the City of London, totaling 4 million square feet. Most of the development is built over the platform and railway tracks of Liverpool Street Station. The multi-use complex expands the financial district of London by providing new office space and trading floors, and enhances the surrounding urban district with retail and leisure facilities. Three public squares and the terraces and landscaping of Exchange Square, with spaces designed for performance and recreation, provide a focal point for the complex.

The 10 buildings are designed in a variety of styles to relate to the city context. Exchange House, at the head of the complex, is a 10-story office block supported on an expressed structural frame arching over the Liverpool Street Station tracks. The buildings facing Bishopsgate present more traditional facades of carved stone and polished granite.

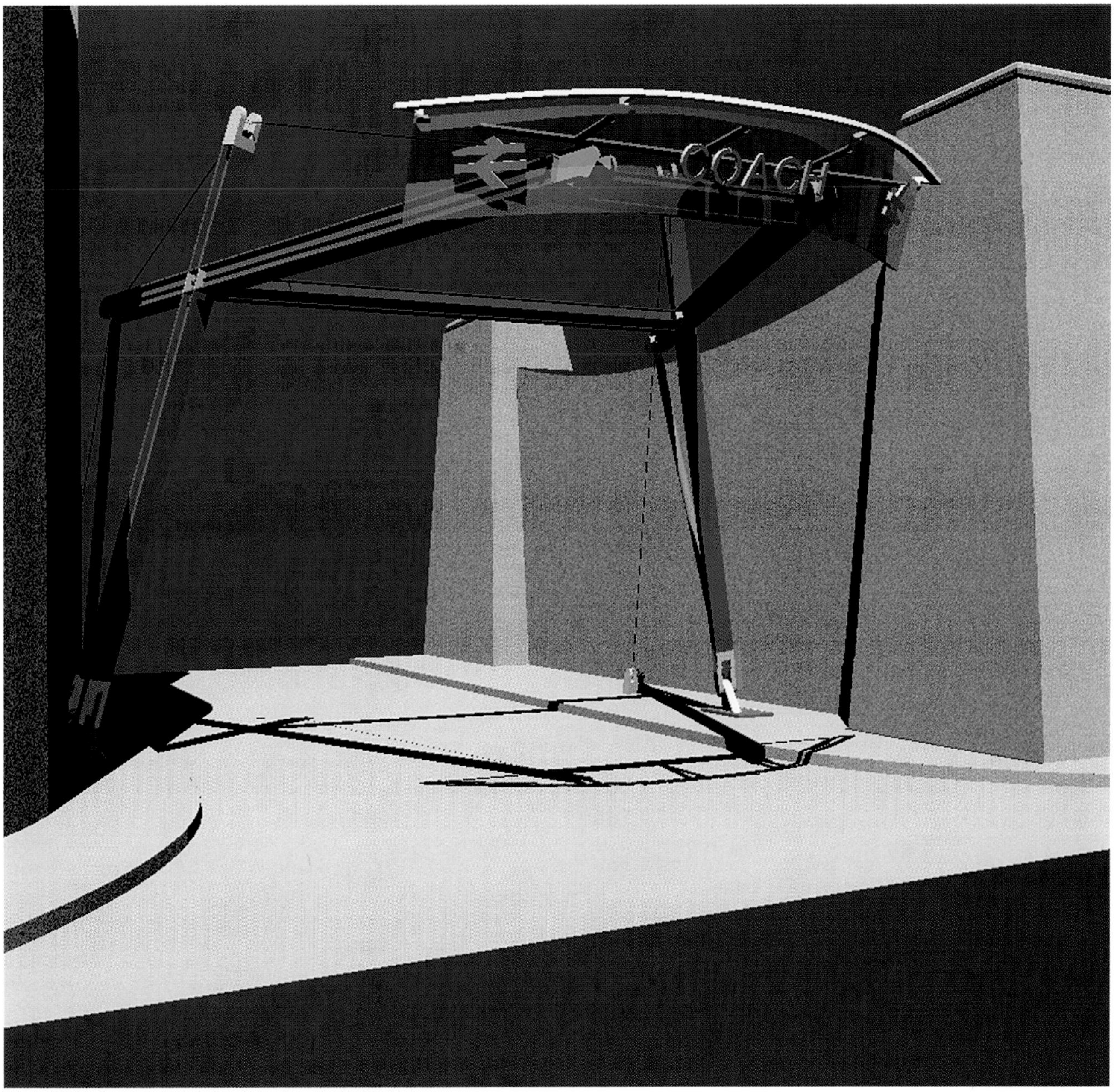

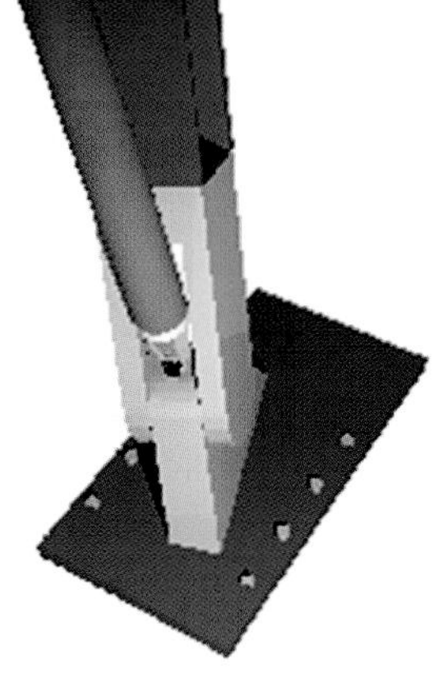

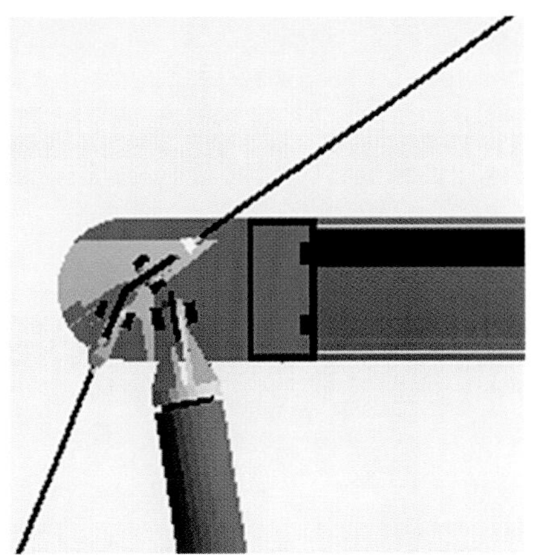

Skidmore, Owings & Merrill

renderers
Nate Kaiser
Mark Allison
Andrew Myren
Steve Burns

World Trade Center

Berlin, Germany

The Berlin World Trade Center was conceived as a complex at the edge of the city, along the canal path in the city's park zone. The project joins a group of significant buildings on the canal path, including the Bauhaus Archive, the National Gallery, and the Philharmonic Orchestra building. Major components of the complex are 36,000 square meters of office space, 7,500 square meters of restaurants and conference center space, 7,100 square meters of residential and hotel accommodations, 175 units of housing, a kindergarten, and parking for 800 cars.

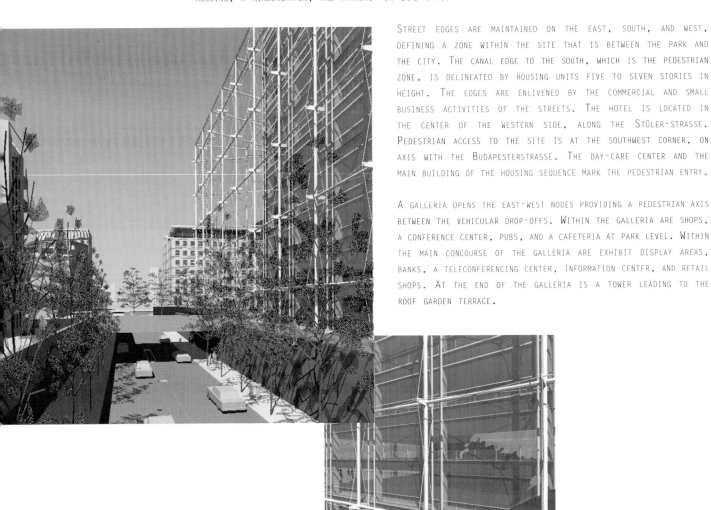

Street edges are maintained on the east, south, and west, defining a zone within the site that is between the park and the city. The canal edge to the south, which is the pedestrian zone, is delineated by housing units five to seven stories in height. The edges are enlivened by the commercial and small business activities of the streets. The hotel is located in the center of the western side, along the Stüler-strasse. Pedestrian access to the site is at the southwest corner, on axis with the Budapesterstrasse. The day-care center and the main building of the housing sequence mark the pedestrian entry.

A galleria opens the east-west nodes providing a pedestrian axis between the vehicular drop-offs. Within the galleria are shops, a conference center, pubs, and a cafeteria at park level. Within the main concourse of the galleria are exhibit display areas, banks, a teleconferencing center, information center, and retail shops. At the end of the galleria is a tower leading to the roof garden terrace.

Skidmore, Owings & Merrill

renderers

Albert Anderson
Mark Schmieding
Nate Kaiser
Steve Hubbard

Jin Mao Building

Shanghai, China

Located in the Pudong District in the city's Lujiazui Finance and Trade Zone, the 265,000-square-meter project is a multi-use development incorporating office, hotel, retail, service amenities, and parking. The tower recalls historic Chinese pagoda forms, with setbacks that create a rhythmic pattern. Its articulated metallic surface captures the sky's movement and light, while at night the shaft and top are illuminated. At 420.5 meters, the tower and its spire are a significant addition to the Shanghai skyline.

The 88-story tower houses hotel and office spaces, with the hotel rooms in the top 38 stories affording impressive views of the city and the surrounding region. Office spaces, in the lower 50 stories, are easily accessed by employees and visitors. Parking for 1,200 cars is located below grade. A seven-story vertical shopping center adjacent to the base of the tower and a landscaped courtyard with reflecting pool and seating at the tower base provide visitors with a peaceful retreat.

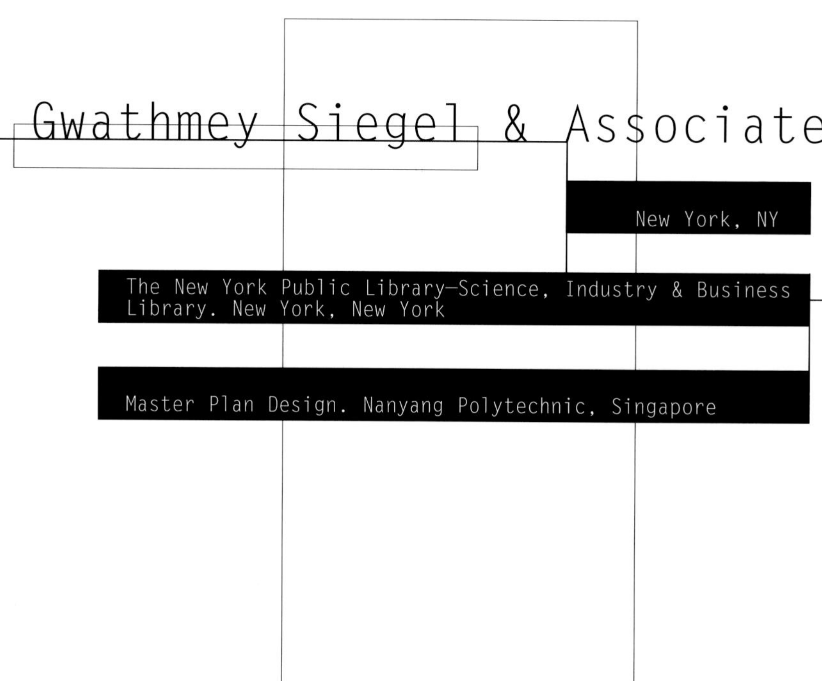

Gwathmey Siegel & Associates
New York, NY
The New York Public Library—Science, Industry & Business Library, New York, New York
Master Plan Design, Nanyang Polytechnic, Singapore

Gwathmey Siegel & Associates was formed in 1968 by Charles Gwathmey and Robert Siegel. The firm has provided professional services for approximately 175 projects. The focus of the firm has been on cultural and educational facilities. The work is internationally respected and has been recognized by numerous publications, exhibitions, and awards including the prestigious American Institute of Architects Firm Award, the New York Chapter of the American Institute of Architects Medal of Honor and the New York State Association of Architects Lifetime Achievement Award.

The Use of Computers at Gwathmey Siegel & Associates

Working together, Charles Gwathmey and Robert Siegel create the initial design strategy for all of the firms projects. Each project is further developed by an associate architect and a team of highly qualified staff architects working closely with both partners until the project is completed. The active involvement of the partners and the continuity of the team enable the firm to produce buildings of the highest caliber.

Gwathmey Siegel architects approach design as an investigative, problem-solving process. Adding computer capabilities to the palette of tools does not alter that process, but rather enhances it. During the beginning phases of design, when the architects investigate a multitude of reiterations and compositions of building elements, computers allow a rapid and exhaustive study, thus a more complete solution.

Computer generated two- and three-dimensional models have become an invaluable visualization tool used as a new combination of perspective and axonometric drawings as well as models, in all phases of design and construction. The first diagrams and models are used as tools to evaluate design. The more-detailed models are employed during design development and construction documentation phases for the detailing and careful study of relationships between building elements. The ease of generating a multitude of views from the same model has also been of great assistance in visualization and in communicating the intentions of the architects to the client.

Computers have provided a tool that was previously unavailable, a tool to study the space and time relationships of design in an unprecedented way: through the use of animated "walk-throughs." For the first time we are able to study movement through time and space in a way that is true to the actual perception of the environment, which has added a new dimension to the perception and visualization of the design possibilities.

The computer-generated models have greatly enhanced the capabilities of studying spatial relationships, implications of different finishes, lighting possibilities, as well as time-space relationships of the design elements. However, there is a drawback in simulating spaces and/or buildings in ways that appear resolved - the impression of a finished design rather than a study model is, at times, seductive. It is important to understand that computer images are design tools or works in progress that offer a more comprehensive evaluation than previous methods of illustration. Used in this context, computers are an invaluable tool.

Gwathmey Siegel & Associates

renderer Elizabeth Skowronek

The New York Public Library—Science, Industry & Business Library

New York, New York

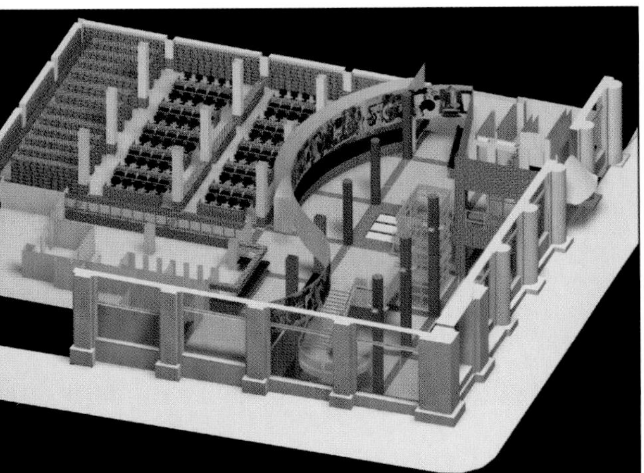

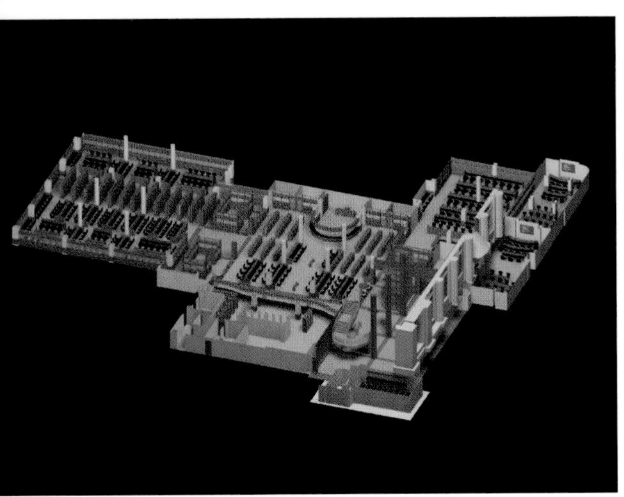

Located in the heart of Manhattan in the skillfully adapted 1906 Renaissance Revival building, formerly home to the fashionable dry-goods emporium of Benjamin Altman, is New York's most important new business and educational resource - the Science, Industry and Business Library (SIBL). Offering free access to over 1.6 million volumes, 60,000 periodicals, and many hundreds of electronic information resources, SIBL represents the Library's response to the changing needs of the city and the nation on the eve of the 21st century.

The challenge posed to the architects was to transform the turn-of-the-century structure into an interactive resource for the Information Age, to retain the structure's classic integrity while incorporating state-of-the-art technology, and to combine the humanistic qualities of traditional libraries with the technology of the future.

SIBL occupies 180,000 square feet of space on more than five levels, at a construction budget of $30 million. It includes major internal structural reconfigurations to accommodate five levels of high-density storage for the collection and a dramatic 33-foot-high entry and exhibition hall. In addition to providing all of the traditional circulating and research library services, the facility offers state-of-the-art information access to international databases free to the public. There are accommodations for electronic data access at all reader stations for laptop computers, as well as dedicated electronic information stations in diverse media and platforms. Taking a cue from the program and the content of the building, the architects employed cutting-edge technology throughout the design and construction phases of the project. Computer-generated drawings were used as the database for the construction; an animated "walk-through" was generated to present the design to the client, and a series of highly detailed interior views were used both as a design tool and to facilitate the client's understanding of the architect's vision. In an apt turn of events, while the structure was being completed, it's digital vision became a part of the "Information Highway." The dramatic volume of the exhibition hall, the comfort of the reading room, and the fluorescent glow of the computer screens in the electronic training center can all be found on the Internet (http://gopher.nypl.org/research/sibl/index.html). The electronic "soul" became a vision of its physical "body."

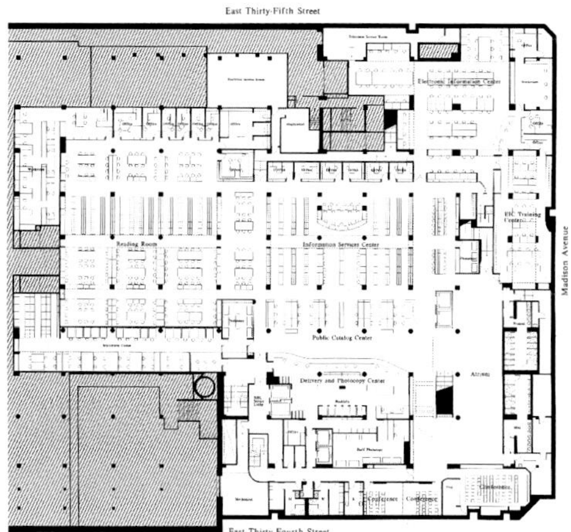

LOWER LEVEL

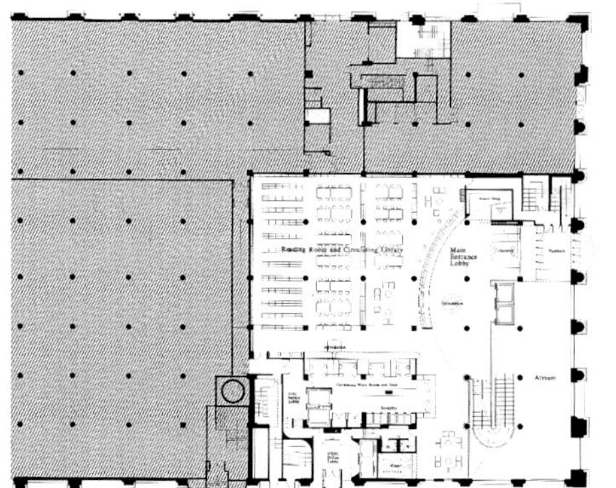

GROUND FLOOR

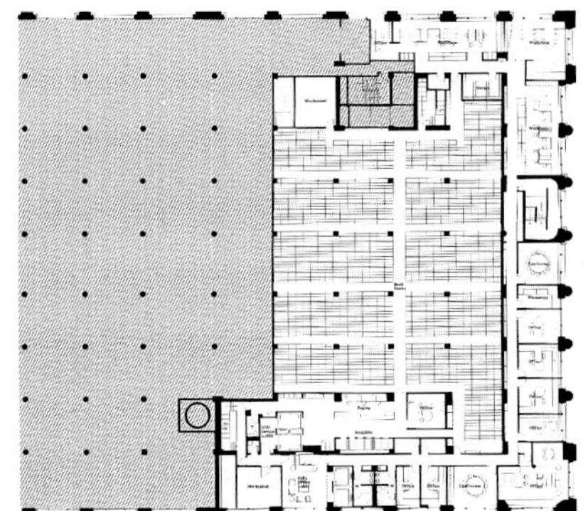

SECOND FLOOR

Gwathmey Siegel & Associates

Master Plan Design
Nanyang Polytechnic

Singapore

renderers
Nelson Benavides
John Hunter
Jay Lampros
George Liaropoulos
Wei-Li Liu
Gregory A. Luhan
Frank Visconti

Nanyang Polytechnic is located on a 75-acre site in north central Singapore. Serving 12,000 students, it is a 2.3-million-square-foot interactive educational community that extends to the north and south from a central multi-use core of common facilities inspired by the "town square" model.

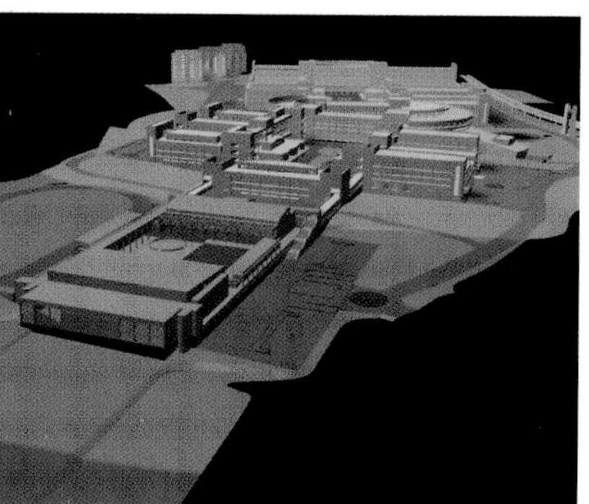

The daily process of arrival, circulation, and return is a designed sequence and procession of varied visual and functional experiences. The overall organization integrates architecture, outdoor space, and pedestrian circulation systems that are psychologically uplifting and inspirational. Circulation is conceived as a circular loop system without dead ends. Multiple options are available, but the primary route from the main entrance to all functions is direct and logical.

A system of cloisters and covered walkways provides access to the four schools as well as all administrative and common-use facilities. The circulation system integrates covered outdoor terraces and is designed to form a series of landscaped outdoor spaces, gardens, and courtyards that offer a multiplicity of visual references and a sense of orientation. The vehicular circulation system is designed to be independent of the pedestrian system and the two never cross without vertical separation.

There are three campus levels sympathetic to the existing topography permitting a balanced program of earth movement. The low level (the western side) provides vehicle access to the School of Engineering, School of Business Management, Main Central Core, and Sports Facilities. The middle level, which includes the Student Activity Center and gardens, provides access to Lecture Theaters, Canteens, Child Care, and Staff Center. The upper level (the eastern side) provides access to the School of Information Technology, School of Health Science, and the Campus Center level 3.

The buildings that house the required program for specific use spaces are efficient, easy to construct, and have logical structures. Exterior facades are a combination of painted stucco and large-scale ceramic tile finish used as a maintenance-oriented lower wall as well as a decorative device to integrate color and texture.

The mission of Nanyang Polytechnic is to bring together business, industry, and education. Its purpose is also to promote intellectual development and reinforce the essential work ethic. The unique appearance and flexible functional characteristics of the Campus Center, the synergistic organization of the campus plan, and the specific program of workshop, Specialist Center, and Industrial Project Center spaces devised for this Polytechnic will provide an environment and image appropriate to meet the challenge of the stated mission.

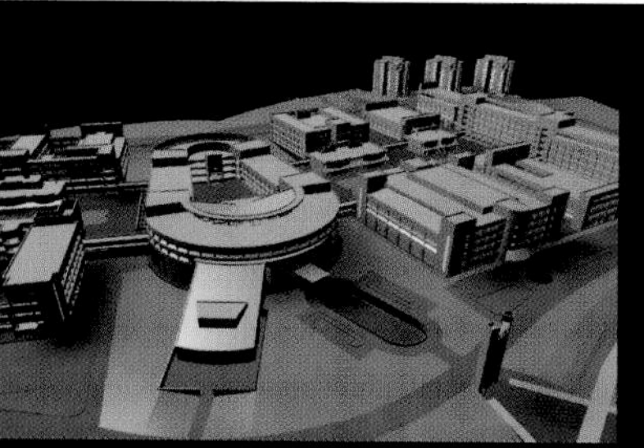

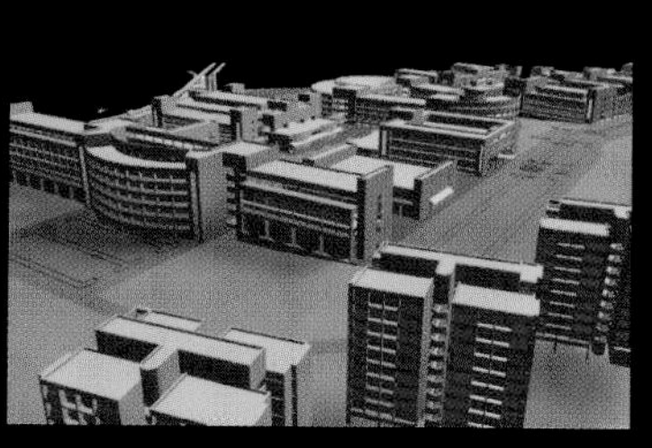

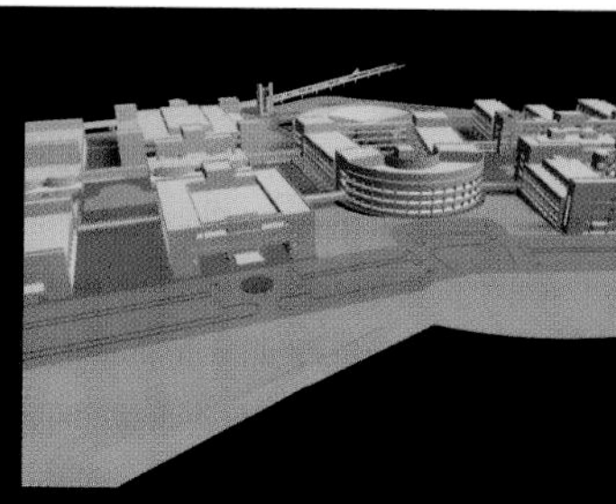

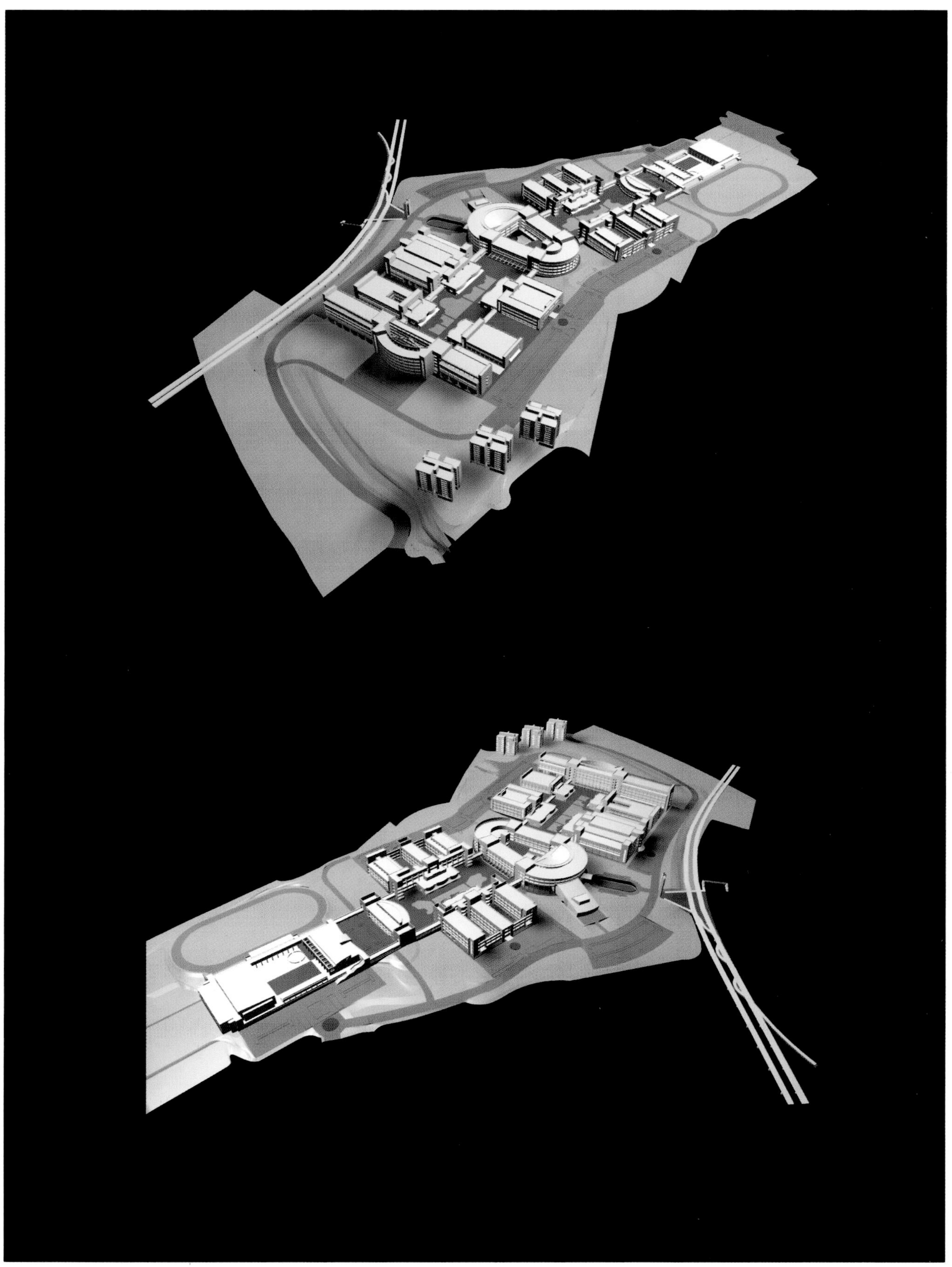

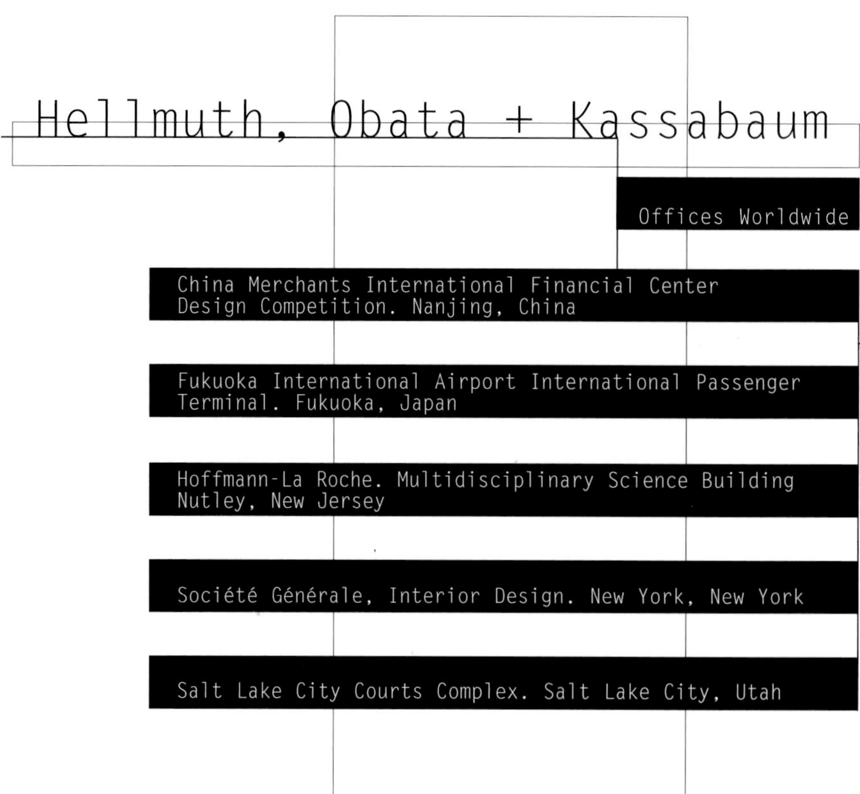

Hellmuth, Obata + Kassabaum
Offices Worldwide
China Merchants International Financial Center Design Competition. Nanjing, China
Fukuoka International Airport International Passenger Terminal. Fukuoka, Japan
Hoffmann-La Roche. Multidisciplinary Science Building Nutley, New Jersey
Société Générale, Interior Design. New York, New York
Salt Lake City Courts Complex. Salt Lake City, Utah

The Use of Computers at Hellmuth, Obata + Kassabaum

Hellmuth, Obata + Kassabaum has maintained its quality design and client service within a team approach, the very philosophy on which the firm was founded by George Hellmuth, Gyo Obata, and George Kassabaum. HOK was established by these three principals in 1955 with a staff of 26 employees. It now includes not only architects, engineers, and planners, but also facilities consultants, specification writers, programmers, construction managers, interior designers, landscape architects, graphic specialists, delineators, and model builders. Its staff of over 1,350 professionals in offices around the globe is experienced in a wide variety of assignments for major corporations, developers, state and local agencies, sports facilities, hospitals, colleges and universities.

Today's rapidly changing information systems have dramatically enhanced HOK's methodology of studying and representing its work. The office-wide strategy is to expand the use of technology in all departments in order to make both the creative and production processes increasingly lean and agile. The firm consistently encourages new methods which inform and shape its work. Although the characteristics of each project vary greatly, they share a common philosophy and strategy in their use of technology.

HOK's philosophy on technology is simple: the most effective technology is transparent. This attitude allows for a clear, uninterrupted focus on project issues throughout the process. The idea is to provide higher quality design through early visualization of concepts and real-world concerns. At every level of project development, tools and presentation methods are critical in representing ideas to clients, consultants, and other design professionals. There is an effort to continue to expand proprietary software, custom tools, and routines through coordination with HOK's Advanced Technology Group. Channels of information between all disciplines are open and there is cross-training through a series of flexible design stations. Several stations have multiplesoftware packages (both HOK-written and off-the-shelf) and are available to all HOK disciplines (such as architecture, engineering, planning, interiors, and graphics). Specific technologies are tailored to the needs of different projects or tasks. This enhances and expedites the decision-making process through the concerted efforts of all linked team members sharing one office-wide database.

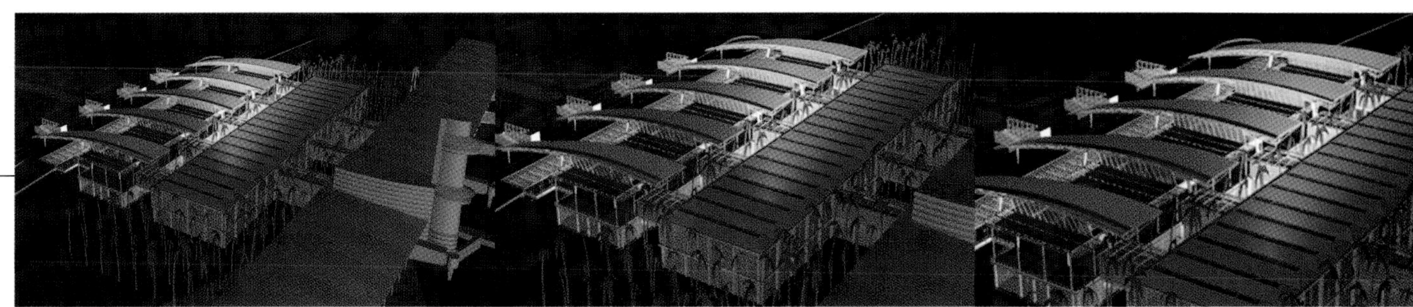

The most recent technological landmark development for HOK has been the release of HOK drawVision. Created by HOK's Advanced Technology Group (ATG), the PC-based program runs on Microsoft Windows NT and uses now-familiar Microsoft Windows' interface. Its capabilities for 2D and 3D are evolving to meet the expanding needs of design as well as production issues. Eventually it will replace HOK Draw, which runs on DEC's VAX 3100 workstations. The obvious advantage of the PC is to have multiple software applications on each machine allowing for greater flexibility per project.

Central to the success of HOK's use of technology is its ability to exchange information with clients, consultants, and other industries. Almost every file type and format can be accommodated at HOK. For example, drawVision has been designed to match all attributes and elements in AutoCAD without compromising drawVision's more advanced approach to CADD. DWG or DXF files can be accepted as well as delivered.

In-house coordination among the various off-the-shelf applications is also crucial. Recent "DXF-out" options in drawVision allow files to be imported into Autodesk's 3D Studio, preserving the original normal and polygonal attributes after triangulation. 3D Studio is being used by designers to study and present projects using ray-tracing, shadow studies, color, texture maps, video animations, and video sketches. Having these tools on several machines provides designers with the necessary palette to investigate architectural concepts as well as present highly detailed photo-realistic images.

New developments are constantly being introduced by HOK Animation. As an integral part of the resources of the firm's Advanced Technology Group, HOK Animation provides animation, video editing, and radiosity capabilities, among others. Using Silicon Graphics hardware and HOK's X-Animate software, 3D data is brought to life and fully animated with lights, materials, colors, and textures. From drawVision, a "save animate" option prepares the data to be imported into X-Animate.

HOK's Radiosity software calculates the emission, reflection, and absorption of light energy and the resulting shadows cast by the surfaces in a closed environment. Radiosity takes the color of a room's light into account so that white light reflecting off a colored surface becomes a colored light source. Radiosity is a dynamic tool for describing space, color, surface, and accessories as realistically as would a full-scale model.

In the very near future, presentations using animations, stills, text, audio- and video-taped interviews will all be on a CD-ROM, placed in a portable laptop, and projected on the wall for client presentations.

Above: Cochin International Airport Design Competition. Cochin, Kerala, India

Hellmuth, Obata + Kassabaum

Donald J. Fedorko
renderer

Nanjing East Road Competition

Nanjing, China

The vision of a vibrant urban space for pedestrians, business exchange, and social activity guided the design of a section of the burgeoning Huangpu District, historically the commercial heart of Shanghai, including much of the city's business, retail, and governmental activity. The concept begins with an internal pedestrian way along the high-traffic intersection of Nanjing and Henan roads. This passage provides linkage to numerous commercial amenities within a five-level, 75,000-square-meter retail center and two office towers, each 40,000 square meters.

The massing of the office tower bases reflects the intense surrounding environment and the area's multiple future developments with a framework for commercial advertising on the wall facing Nanjing Road. The urban grid is reinforced by the massing, while the structure's curved facades on the block's inner side emphasize views up and down Nanjing Road. Shadowing on blocks to the north is also minimized by the towers' massing concept.

Hellmuth, Obata + Kassabaum

Michael Sechman
renderer

Fukuoka International Airport International Passenger Terminal

Fukuoka, Japan

The gently curved roof of the 66,042-square-meter terminal is divided into five air-foil-like shells that hover above the main departure level. Like wings of an airplane taking off, the leading edges are lifted toward the airside capturing north light and glimpses of sky for passengers in the ticketing areas on the departure level. The design of concourses and arrivals areas all draw from concepts initiated in the departure hall roof. Orientation to the spine and clarifying circulation are key to the success of this design.

The supporting structure is exposed tube steel that forms lines of floor-to-ceiling composite trusses running east/west under the clerestories. This design allows for the large 10-meter overhangs on the east and west as well as a column-free "spine" in the center. Four-column clusters along the landside road to the south and along the airside edge of the ticket hall to the north buttress the structure from the earthquakes and wind forces in the north/south direction.

Japan Airlines
Japan Airlines
ANA

Hellmuth, Obata + Kassabaum

David Munson
renderer

Hoffmann-La Roche Multidisciplinary Science Building

Nutley, New Jersey

Hoffmann-La Roche retained HOK to design a flexible technical facility on a complex multifunctional site in Nutley, New Jersey. In response to the requirements, the Multidisciplinary Science Building organizes and strengthens the images and identities of the research, manufacturing, and administration functions on the Nutley campus. It links research functions on the site for greater interaction, while allowing for future site development and integrates space for laboratories and related process development areas in the same facility. These improvements respect the existing fabric of the campus, enhance the campus setting, and create an image reflecting the importance of Hoffmann-La Roche's commitment to R & D.

The Multidisciplinary Science Building is a six-story modular research building consisting of four laboratory wings organized along a central spine. A conference center along this artery makes the new Science Building the heart of the campus research community. The large floor plan permits flexibility in accommodating changing space needs of different-sized research groups.

The facility houses 408 laboratory and process modules including molecular biology research, pharmaceutical R & D, and process development areas fostering a team approach from exploratory research through early product development, which helps Roche speed new therapies to market. While easily accessible to the interior street, the lab wings are deliberately designed as dead ends in order to eliminate through traffic.

The Science Building is not designed to make an architectural statement; its design is derived from the existing visual context of the campus. The quiet nature of the exterior, along with the open space the building creates, allows the nearby corporate headquarters building to retain its visual importance on the campus.

Hellmuth, Obata + Kassabaum

David Munson
renderer

Société Générale

New York, New York

Société Générale, an international banking institution headquartered in Paris, recently centralized their various New York offices into new space. They have grown substantially over the past years, and this relocation afforded a rare opportunity to redefine the physical organization of their work environment.

HOK provided Société Générale with an architectural expression of their progressive thinking, creating spaces that are well-designed and elegant, without being ostentatious. Their offices are centralized and organized to provide a cohesive way of working.

Special features of this project include a 3,500-square-foot data center and a 225-post trading floor, plus the dedicated emergency generators and cooling tower necessary to guarantee uninterrupted power to these spaces. Other amenities include executive offices, executive dining room, and an employee training center.

Because of the fast-tracked schedule, HOK established an ambitious schedule for meetings with the top level management of Société Générale: meetings with the CEO and the deputy managing director occured at least weekly; and the lengthy meetings with the chief financial officer occured at least twice each week. The project required the highest level of participation and commitment from Société Générale and HOK, and consensus building and decision making were greatly facilitated.

Hellmuth, Obata + Kassabaum

Michael Sechman
renderer

Salt Lake City Courts Complex

Salt Lake City, Utah

The most significant challenge of this prestigious national design competition was the creation of an architectural expression that appropriately reflects the dignity and gravity of the court system. Additionally, this project needed to reflect the traditions of Salt Lake architecture. Located on one of the city's most prominent sites, it was required to be properly integrated into the city's urban master plan.

Particularly important was development of the proper functional relationships in the large floor plate made necessary by site and urban design conditions. Also, the respective pairing of state supreme and appellate, district and magistrate, family and juvenile, arraignment and high security courts presented further challenges, in addition to meeting the state's budget of less than $72 million, or no more than $117 per gross square foot (far below comparable projects nationwide).

HOK's solution for this unique six-week competition was unanimously selected by a wide margin over other schemes. The 420,000-square-foot complex includes 38 courts and associated administrative and support spaces for the clerks of the court, law libraries, public and private dining, conference center, and the sheriff's department. The T-shaped pedestrian spine on the ground level, with the rotunda as its hub, provides easy circulation for the offices and courts with the same concept followed throughout the building. The floor plates are designed for 16 courts and exceed the efficiency of the state's program. In addition, HOK's design incorporates future expansion for additional courtrooms.

HOK uses imagery which evokes civic authority and judicial presence, combined with the desire to relate to the surrounding structures. This is a modern building with classical attributes and proportions. The exterior is faced in traditional limestone and detailed in a fashion which emulates great civic structures while clearly expressing its contemporary attitude. HOK's design balances the needs of the court for both image and security. It responds to the city context of an adjacent historical government building, and a location with primary views of the state capitol. HOK has furthered the city's goals by complementing the scale of nearby buildings and creating a mid-block passage through the site.

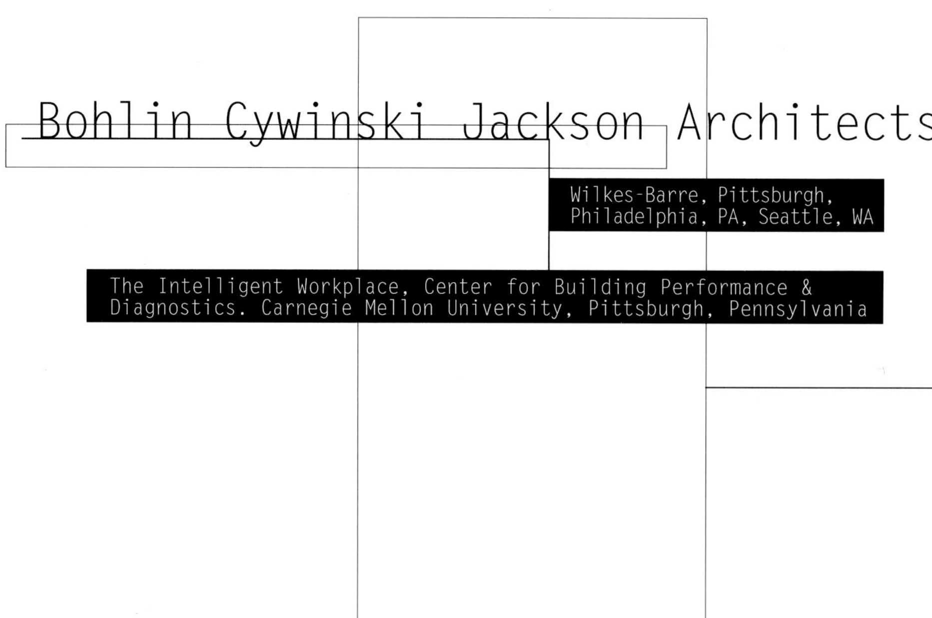

Bohlin Cywinski Jackson Architects
Wilkes-Barre, Pittsburgh,
Philadelphia, PA, Seattle, WA
The Intelligent Workplace, Center for Building Performance &
Diagnostics. Carnegie Mellon University, Pittsburgh, Pennsylvania

Bohlin Cywinski Jackson offers services in architecture, planning, and interior design and now has offices in Wilkes-Barre, Pittsburgh, Philadelphia, and Seattle. Organized as a professional corporation, the firm has five principals and ten associates with a total staff of approximately 55. The firm has developed a reputation for design excellence evidenced by more than 110 regional, national, and international awards earned by the firm, and through extensive publication of its work in professional journals worldwide.

The Use of Computers at Bohlin Cywinski Jackson Architects

Bohlin Cywinski Jackson's approach to CAD & visualization with computers has been a deliberate series of small but incremental steps. This approach has been driven by both economics and design priorities. Generally, our incremental approach affords a healthy evaluation of new electronic tools without sacrificing design quality.

Beginning in the late 1980s, a number of BCJ staff members began advocating the GUI-based Apple Macintosh and its intuitive software applications. Starting with Claris CAD and Modelshop, BCJ Pittsburgh's staff began to explore ways to exploit these basic tools. The general philosophy was to emphasize simplicity and ease of use over more feature-rich applications. Once staff were comfortable with the basics, the complexity and extent of the work accomplished via computer was slowly increased. The next generation of CAD applications, FlexiCAD and Form•Z are still in use today in three offices. FlexiCAD is installed on about 30 '040 Mac workstations. Form•Z is installed on only a couple of workstations in each office, reflecting the slower adaptation to 3D modeling techniques.

The circumstance of the project drives the degree to which computer visualization is used. Often, projects that are more rational and technology intensive, such as laboratories, have benefited most. BCJ attempts to use computer-based solutions when they fit the solution or when the opportunity to push the technology and skills further is feasible within the project budget.

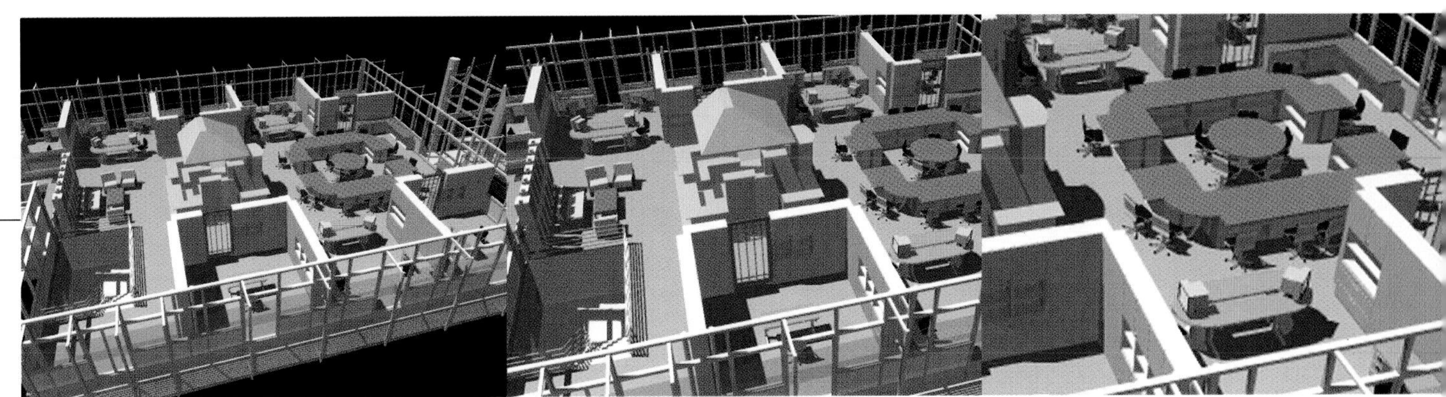

As with the diverse character of its architecture, BCJ relies on a diversity of methods for design and presentations. Sometimes CAD is substituted for traditional models, but more often it is used as an aid in perspective generation or to create QuickTime walk-throughs.

Another important impact is easier production of marketing/publication drawings and new media such as video, computer film clips, etc. "After the fact" presentations for awards programs are easily filtered out of CAD files, usually using software such as Freehand, Canvas, or Claris CAD. These drawings replace the traditional ink on mylar figurative plans, sections, and axonometrics.

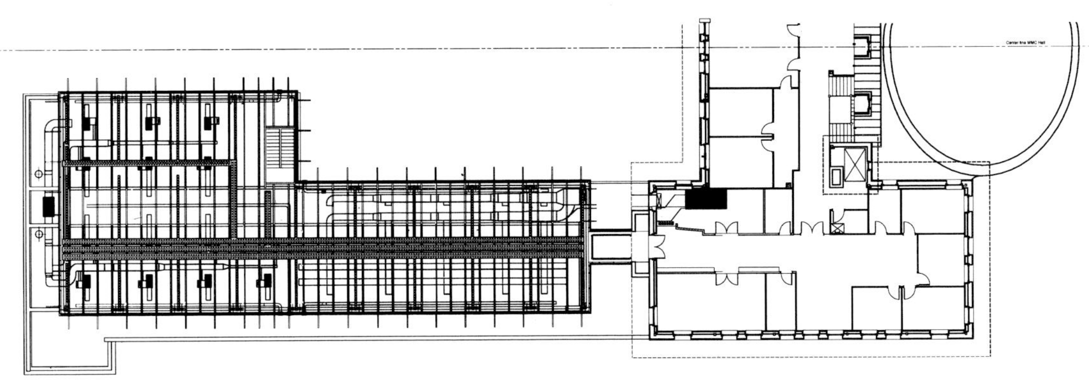

Bohlin Cywinski Jackson Architects

renderer Azizan Aziz, CMU

The Intelligent Workplace, Center for Building Performance & Diagnostics

Carnegie Mellon University,
Pittsburgh, Pennsylvania

The Intelligent Workplace is a long-term demonstration, research, and teaching project for the Advanced Building Systems Integration Consortium (ABSIC). The university-industry consortium consists of 10 major U.S. building industries, Carnegie Mellon, and the National Science Foundation. The envisioned structure, which will be constructed on the roof of Margaret Morrison Carnegie Hall (designed by Henry Hornbostel) will enable interchangeability and side-by-side demonstrations of innovations in HVAC, enclosure, interior, and telecommunications systems.

In addition to the primary research focus, the project also must successfully fit into the surrounding environment of the historic building upon which it is sited as well as the surrounding campus. By breaking the massing of the 6,000-square-foot structure into a series of modular bays that support asymmetrical sawtooth/hipped roof configurations, the roof form not only maximizes solar orientation, but also creates a breakdown in scale sympathetic with the roofscape of the campus.

The internal planning is conceptualized as an "intelligent village" that maximizes interaction while retaining opportunities for the occupant to withdraw into "coves" of greater privacy. Working with major vendors of workstation technology, the Center hopes to test new work group configurations and provide feedback to manufacturers on how to more fully integrate their products with HVAC, lighting, and ergonomic technologies. Another major feature of the interior plan is the "service pub" which is designed to address the integration of the traditional social places in the work environment with removal of exhaust by-products of office equipment.

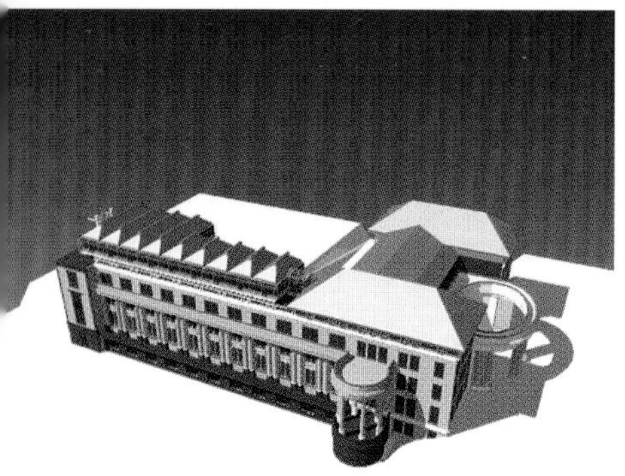

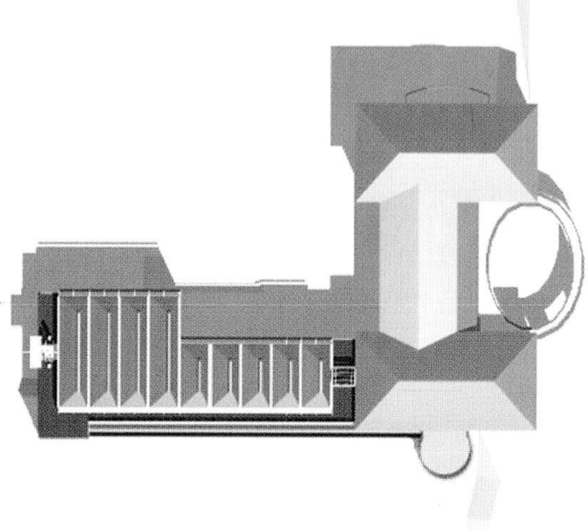

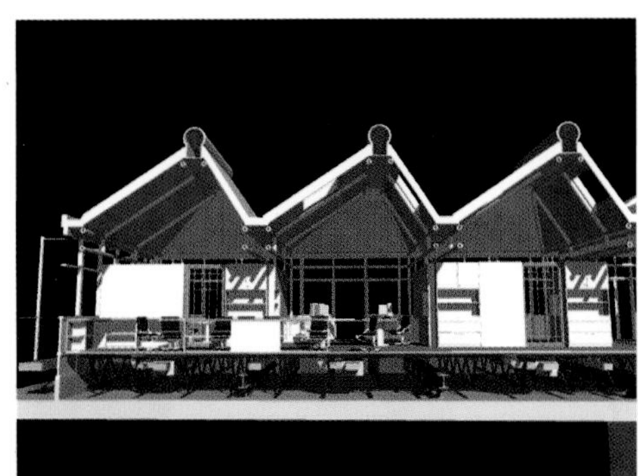

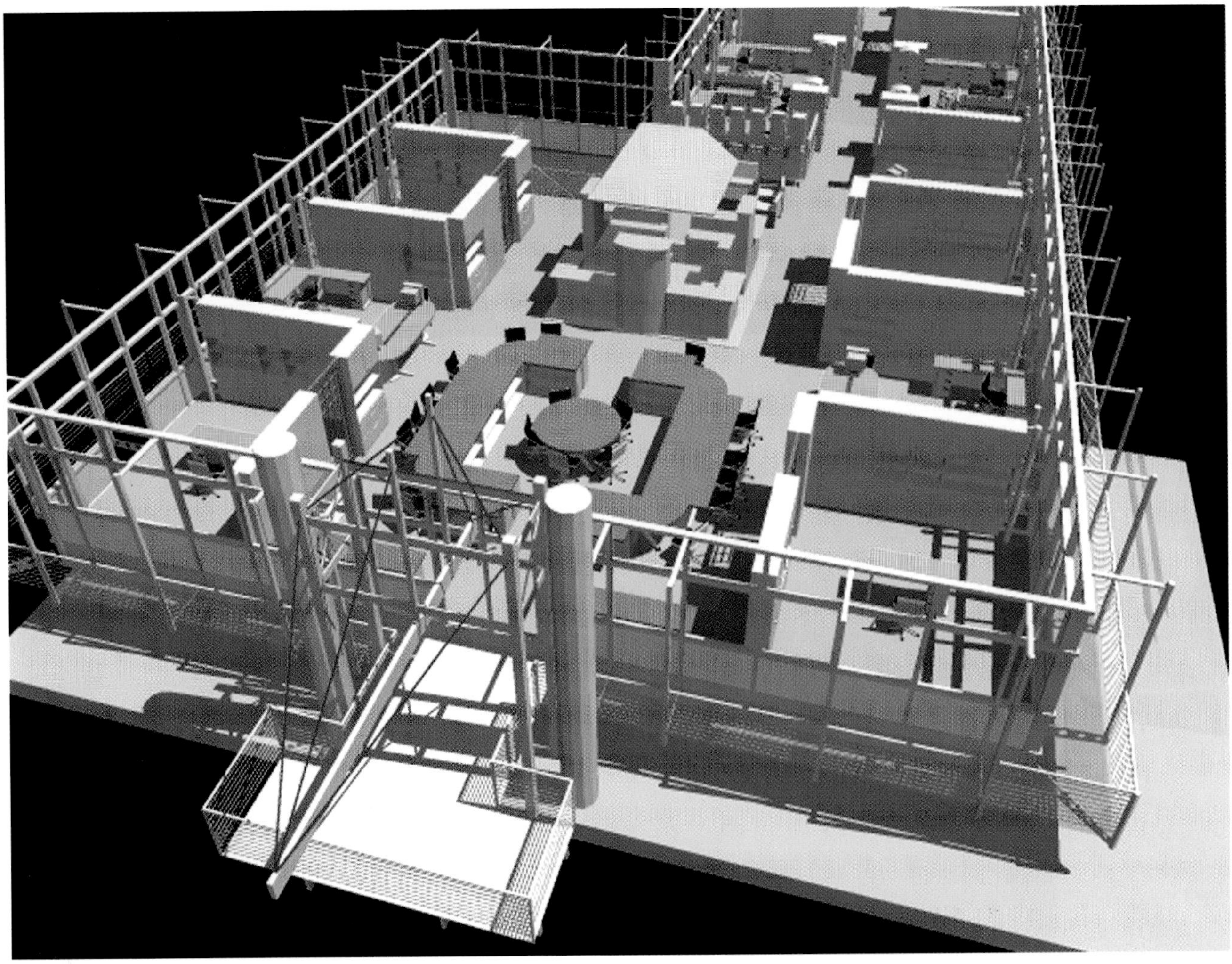

Constructability was studied at the earliest stages of the design by modeling the building components and simulating their assembly through computer animation. The images below illustrate the construction sequence; the roof reinforcing "chassis", the floor sub-structure, the roof super-structure, the building envelope, and the mechanical/electrical systems. The structural components, a "kit of parts", are mass produced in the shop and assembled in the field using bolted connections for speed and efficiency. The design was further refined by working directly with the steel fabricator to make the system lighter and easier to produce and install.

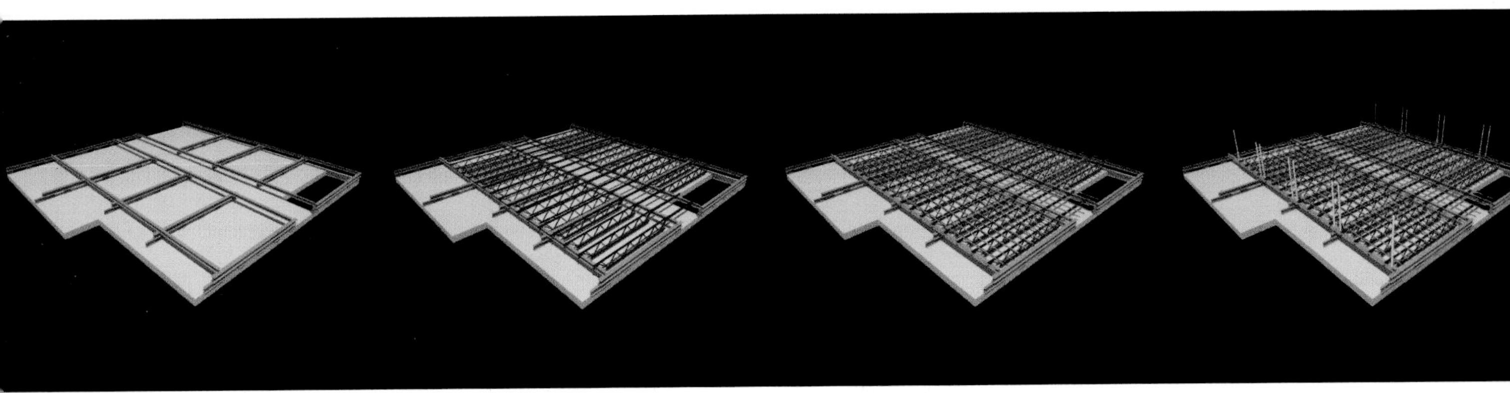

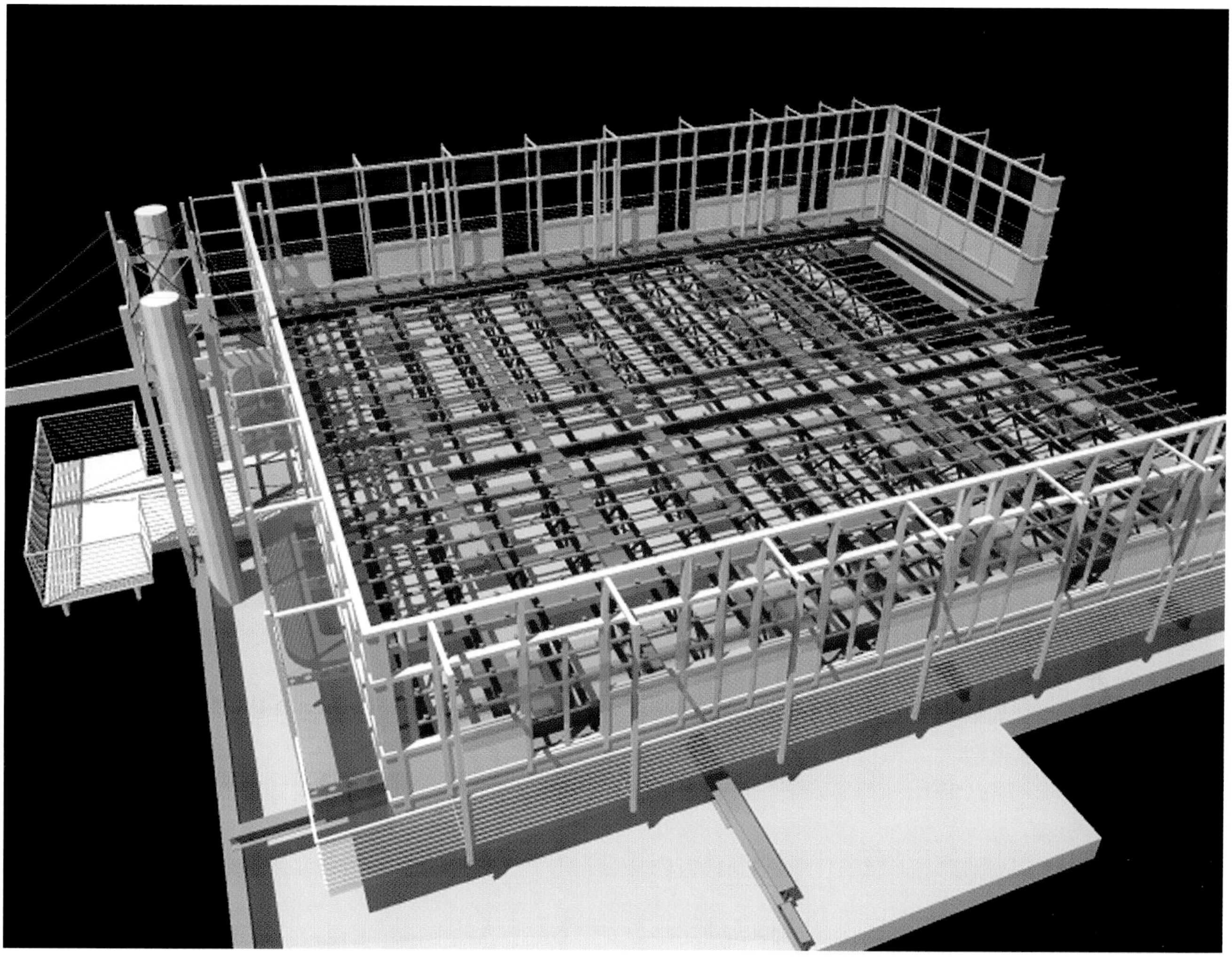

The dynamic, multi-layered envelope system is hung from the structure with custom sliding brackets that allow the facade to move independently of the structure when subjected to differential thermal stress. Programmable light-redirection louvers are mounted on the service catwalk. These louvers sense the ambient light levels within the work environment and respond by reflecting additional sunlight into the room when it is needed.

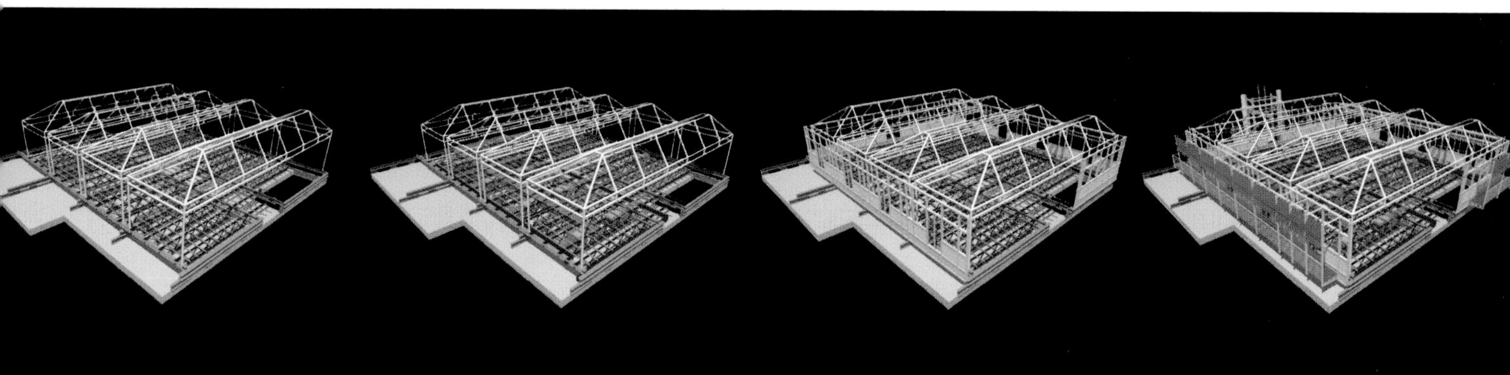

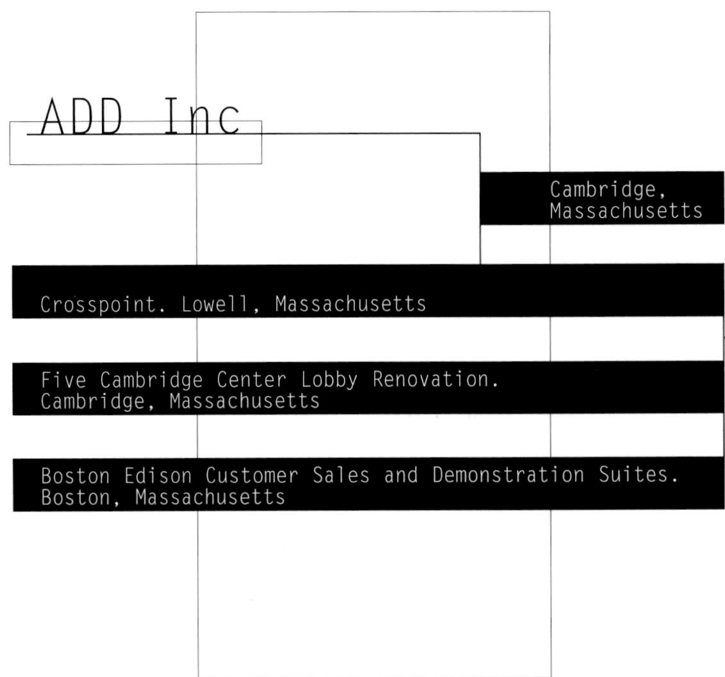

ADD Inc
Cambridge, Massachusetts
Crosspoint. Lowell, Massachusetts
Five Cambridge Center Lobby Renovation. Cambridge, Massachusetts
Boston Edison Customer Sales and Demonstration Suites. Boston, Massachusetts

ADD Inc is a 70-person architectural, interior design, planning, and consulting firm founded in 1971 in Cambridge, Massachusetts, that provides design services nationwide for corporations, public agencies, retail, residential, and institutional clients. In addition, ADD Inc Retail Strategies Group provides advisory services to developers, owners, and investors of retail properties. A second initiative, Applied, specializes in software for facilities management.

The Use of Computers at Architecture Design Development

The sophistication of ADD Inc's computer system gives the firm the capability to provide clients with a wide range of architecturally-related services and products. Everyone in the firm, from principals to administrative staff, has a networked computer and the turnaround time for drawings, specifications, graphical and marketing materials of consistent, high quality is, thereby, markedly reduced. A broad range of software applications - sophisticated 3D modeling, computer-aided design, spreadsheets, desktop publishing, and presentation software have been integrated into a single seamless system. Design drawings, charts, photographs, maps, logos, text, and numerical information are readily accessible and easily manipulated. Further, because the firm's operators are architects and designers - not merely skilled technicians - ADD Inc renderings are innovative and creative.

Like most architecture firms and their engineering counterparts, ADD Inc at first used computers primarily for the production of construction documents and found, like most design professionals, that there is a decided advantage to computer drawing over hand drawing. However, as the firm became proficient and as individuals became familiar with the machine, it became abundantly clear that there was great potential yet to be realized. ADD Inc began to use the computer as a design tool. With software such as Virtus Walkthrough and Alias Upfront, 3D drawings were produced to facilitate decision making and to present design options to clients.

ADD Inc has begun to experiment with evocative 2D images and sophisticated, rendered 3D models in a concerted effort to utilize the computer as a design tool. The intention is to provide an opportunity for office-wide involvement in this endeavor with a view toward better design. It is well established that representation both reflects and influences the way a society understands the world and the decisions it makes in that world. Just as the "discovery" of mathematical perspective symbolized the world view of Renaissance

culture and thereby established the limits of the possible, computers will circumscribe the boundaries of our participation in the creative act. Designers cannot abdicate to computers (or to any other mechanism) the responsibility incumbent upon them to exercise the reasonable and sensitive judgment that is the essence of design.

Above: (top) *66 Summer Street. Boston, Massachusetts.* (bottom) *2 Devonshire Street. Boston, Massachusetts.*

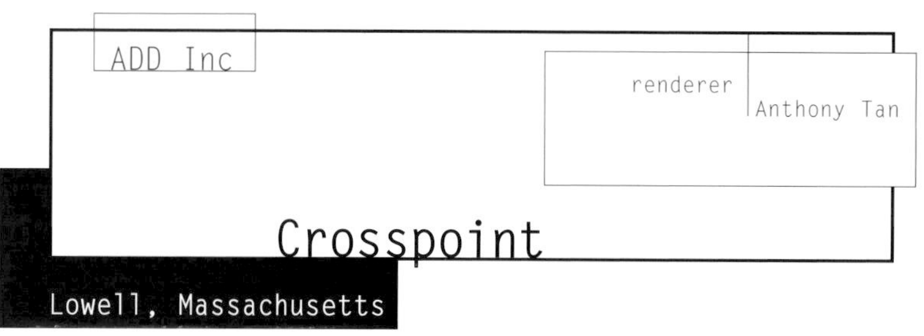

ADD Inc

renderer Anthony Tan

Crosspoint

Lowell, Massachusetts

Cross Point is a million-square-foot office building consisting of three 13-story towers that are interconnected by vertical mechanical cores. The office complex had previously been a corporate headquarters for a high-tech corporation.

The new owners recognized the need to upgrade and transform the architectural character of the existing buildings. ADD Inc's charge was to design a new entry, and to alter the infrastructure and the public spaces, enhancing the character of the buildings by re-configuring the interior spaces at ground level.

Two new ground-level entrance lobbies were created. These are connected by a broad gallery whose edges are enlivened by new tenant amenities such as small retail shops and a health club. The lobby spaces were conceived to be light-filled spaces anchoring both ends of this corridor, piercing the opaque exterior of the buildings. Pieces of the lobby curtainwall were distorted into complex geometrical forms to animate the building facade and allow glimpses of the renovated landscape from the new lobbies.

ADD Inc

renderer Anthony Tan

Boston Edison Customer Sales and Demonstration Suites

Boston, Massachusetts

The Boston Edison Project is a 50,000-square-foot interior design for the largest electric utility in Massachusetts – a renovation of two floors at the Prudential Tower. The focus of the project is a Customer Sales and Demonstration suite where new energy products and systems are demonstrated to corporate executives, architects, and engineers.

The design attempts to showcase the emergence of Boston Edison as a progressive and technologically advanced company. Not only are the products and programs on display, so also is the lighting. Lighting is used effectively throughout to manipulate one's perception of the architecture. The lighting solutions are, therefore, unusual and diverse, and a powerful vehicle for the image of an electric utility.

A visitor's first impression as the elevator doors open is the gentle arc of a translucent glass wall backlighted by low voltage fixtures to animate the wall and light the entry softly. The arc inflects the shallow space at the elevator lobby towards the conference and demonstration areas. At the reception desk, exposed light fixtures are used to highlight rich, but minimal, natural materials of wood, glass, and metal. The linear cold cathode element above the desk visually links the reception area to the display area, passing through the "fishbowl" conference room.

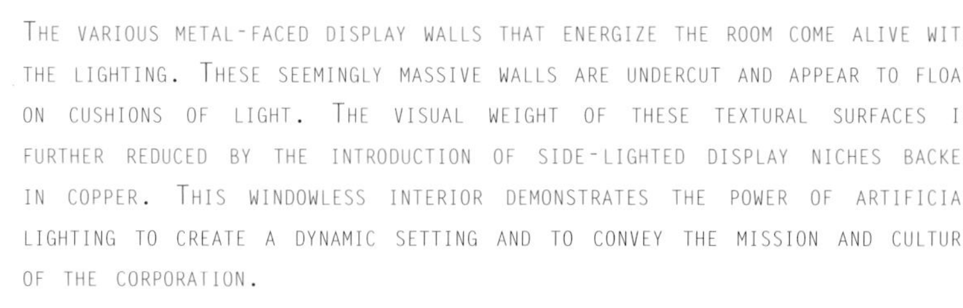

The various metal-faced display walls that energize the room come alive with the lighting. These seemingly massive walls are undercut and appear to float on cushions of light. The visual weight of these textural surfaces is further reduced by the introduction of side-lighted display niches backed in copper. This windowless interior demonstrates the power of artificial lighting to create a dynamic setting and to convey the mission and culture of the corporation.

ADD Inc

renderer Anthony Tan

Five Cambridge Center Lobby Renovation

Cambridge, Massachusetts

The project is the renovation of a 6,000-square-foot lobby for a 232,000-square-foot office building at Cambridge Center. The existing building helped to spearhead the redevelopment of the Kendall Square/MIT area of East Cambridge in the early 1980s. The original lobby was modernist in conception as an extension of the sidewalk and plaza outside. As development in the area over the last decade produced surrounding buildings with ever more "refined" treatment, the need to renovate this space became clear. There were yet other reasons to rethink the design of the original lobby: the circulation was ill-conceived, there was no seating, and the space was dominated by a poorly located reception desk.

The design challenge was to make the lobby an appropriate anteroom to the first-class office space, to clarify the circulation, and to relocate the reception desk so that it addresses both entrances equally. These goals were constrained by the condition that the window wall could not be altered.

The design sets a new threshold within the space, free of the curtain-wall, to demarcate the passage from the "sidewalk" to the first-class office space. This intervention introduces a new geometry that inflects the space to unify the seating, reception, and elevator lobby and to clarify the circulation.

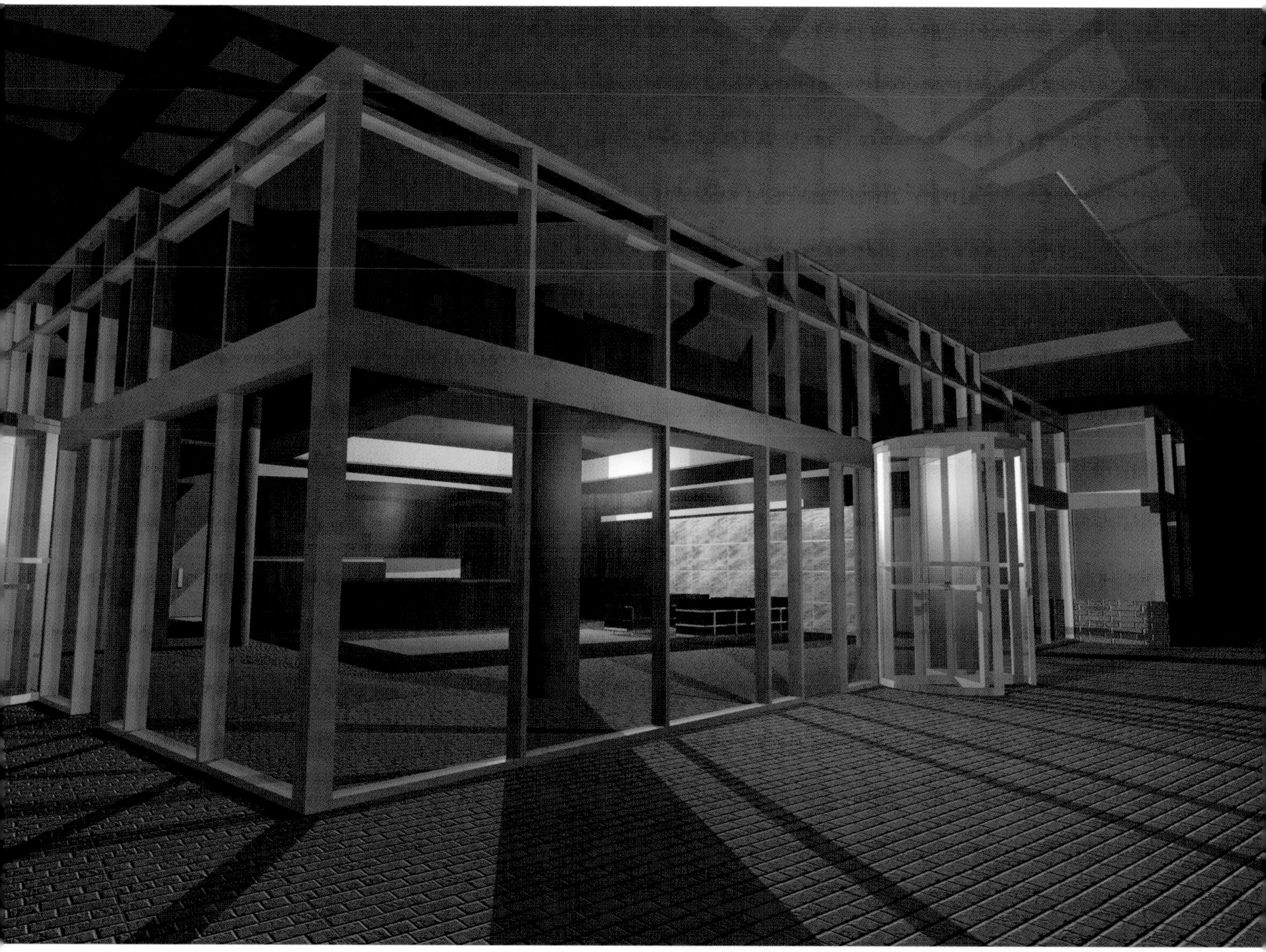

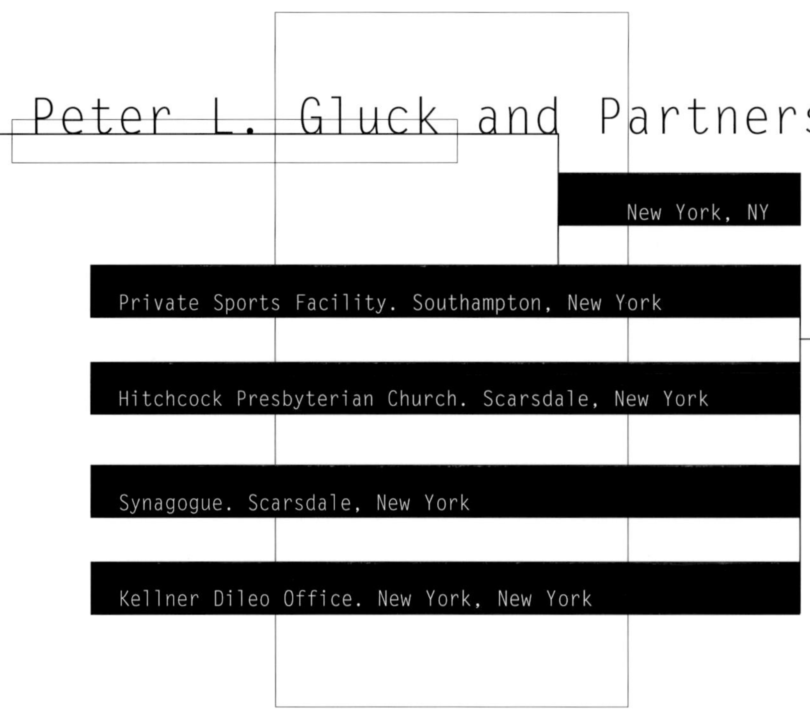

Peter L. Gluck and Partners
New York, NY
Private Sports Facility. Southampton, New York
Hitchcock Presbyterian Church. Scarsdale, New York
Synagogue. Scarsdale, New York
Kellner Dileo Office. New York, New York

Peter L. Gluck and Partners, a New York-based architectural firm, has designed buildings for a wide range of public and private clients for over 20 years. Major projects include hotels, schools, religious buildings, private residences, and corporate interiors. The firm's projects have involved historic restoration and adaptive reuse of historic structures, planning, and construction management.

The Use of Computers at Peter L. Gluck and Partners

A staff of between 15 and 20 architects works on the firm's projects. Particular focus over the years has been on cost control, construction quality, and the craft of building. Several works in progress are being constructed by AR/CS, a construction management firm allied to Peter L. Gluck.

Kent Larson, partner-in-charge of the work shown in these pages, has led the exploration of computer graphics techniques as a tool in the design process. The firm's use of the computer differs from how most firms use this technology in a number of ways.

Whereas most firms use digital technology primarily for 2D drafting, computer graphics at Peter Gluck and Partners is used mainly for 3D modeling and rendering. The scale and complexity of most of their projects makes manual drafting often more efficient, and makes 3D computer graphic simulation ideal.

Most firms use 3D modeling and rendering primarily for presentations in lieu of traditional hand-drawn perspectives. Peter Gluck and Partners use this digital technology primarily in-house for design study and evaluation, and for the development of conceptual/analytical images. Traditional media and abstract digital imagery is more often used for client presentations. The firm has found that photo-realistic images at the schematic and design development phase are often inappropriate and misleading to clients.

The firm uses sophisticated lighting simulation software and high-end UNIX workstations found in few architectural offices, and has no specialized computer operators. Architects themselves use the computers.

The firm has been able to assemble digital tools seldom found in an architectural firm of this size due in large part to Larson's work and articles outside of the practice. He has received two grants from the Graham Foundation for Advanced Studies in the Fine Arts for the digital investigation of unbuilt architecture. This has led to collaborative relationships with companies such as Silicon Graphics, Autodesk, Adobe, Integra, Lightscape, and Sigma Design.

This Page: *Pavilions and Pool at a Mies van der Rohe House*

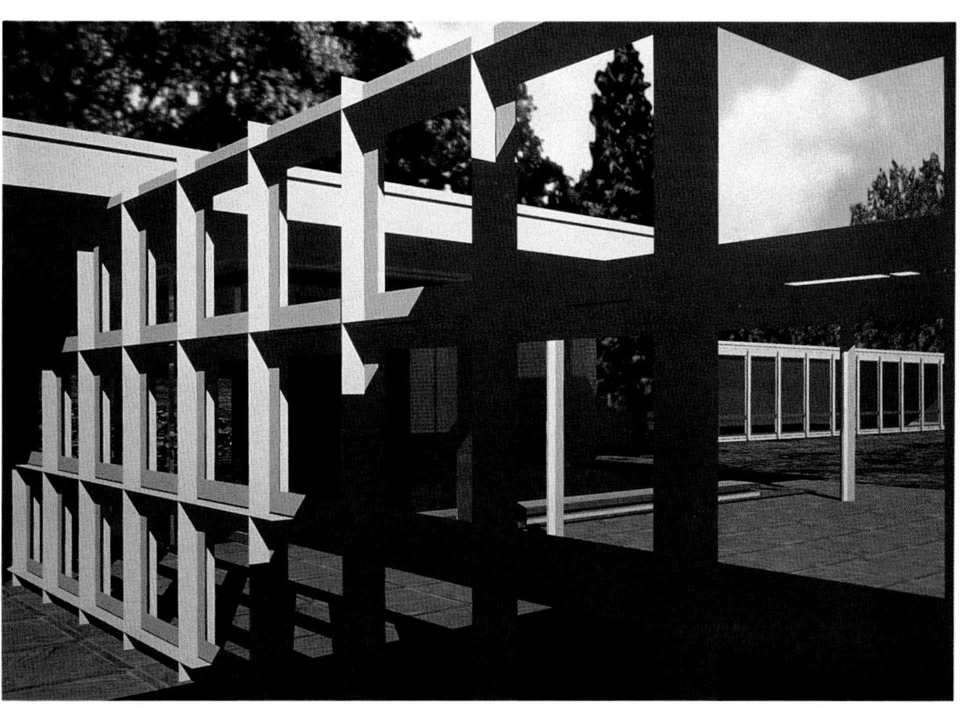

Peter L. Gluck and Partners

renderer/partner-in-charge
Kent Larson

Private Sports Facility

Southampton, New York

The program for this private sports facility is similar to the "playhouse" of the turn of the century - a sports related building within a family compound adjacent to the living spaces. The building, several hundred feet from the family's main home, contains a gymnasium, squash court, climbing wall, sauna, steam room, lap pool, billiard area, and dance space. Also included is a private owner's apartment with a view of the entire estate in the north wing, and a caretaker's apartment in the south wing. Each wing is separated by an 18-foot-high open breezeway covered by a long pitched roof. To minimize the scale of this 22,000-square-foot building in the heart of Southampton's residential area, the gym, squash court, and locker rooms are placed below grade. The lap pool is a "lantern" bringing light to the lower level with 4"-thick underwater windows.

The image of two exterior elevations presented to the community is that of a rural barn. Exterior materials are mahogany windows, cedar shingles and siding, tinted stucco, and copper trim - surfaces that will weather naturally in the salt air.

The interior is a complex series of spaces rendered in steel, concrete, stone, plaster, and oak. Large structural steel trusses frame the 45-foot-high gymnasium, and support a large cantilevered roof.

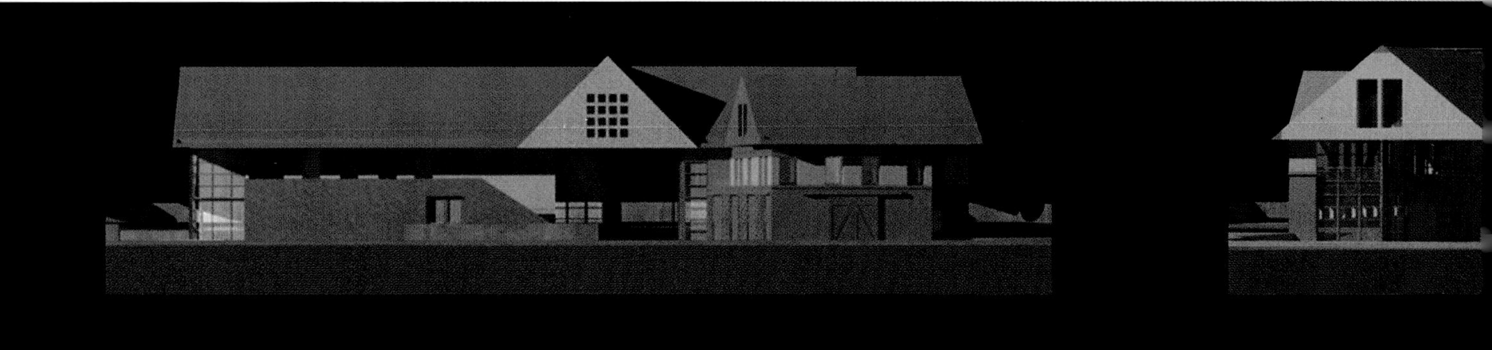

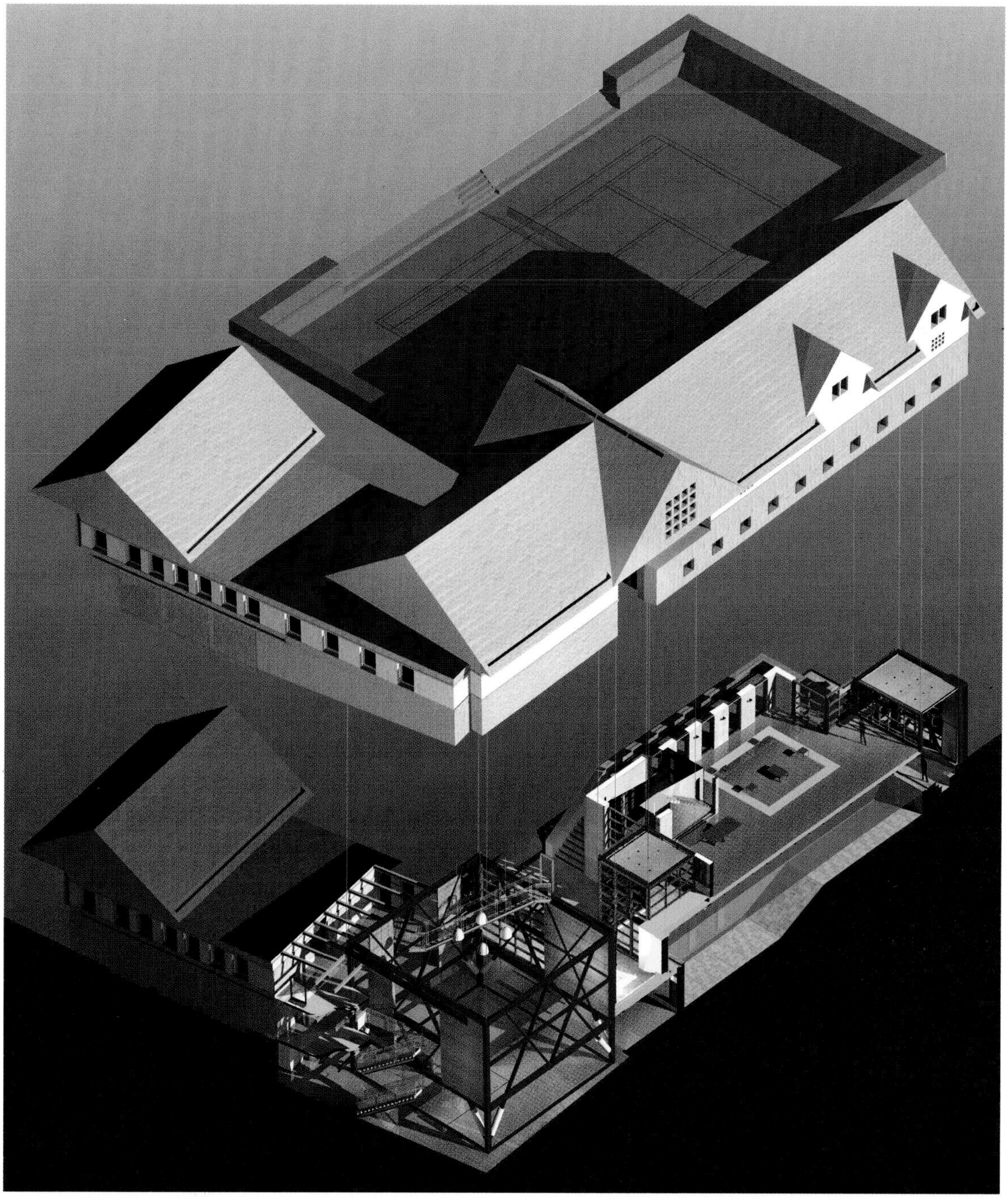

Peter L. Gluck and Partners

renderer/partner-in-charge
Kent Larson

Hitchcock Presbyterian Church

Scarsdale, New York

With the destruction by arson of an old sanctuary, the congregation took the opportunity to reevaluate its needs. They determined that a new sanctuary should be larger, have excellent acoustics, and should be more open and brighter than the old with its dark wood, small windows, and low ceilings. It was important that the new church should be sensitive to the scale and character of the surrounding neigh-

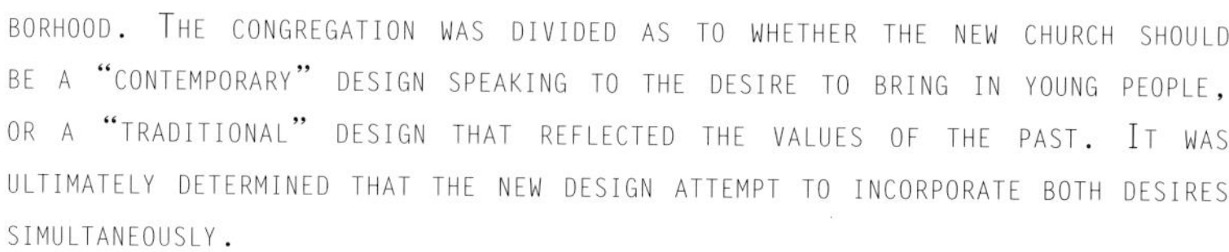
borhood. The congregation was divided as to whether the new church should be a "contemporary" design speaking to the desire to bring in young people, or a "traditional" design that reflected the values of the past. It was ultimately determined that the new design attempt to incorporate both desires simultaneously.

The Norman-inspired granite bell tower and buttresses were all that remained after the fire, and these were incorporated into the new sanctuary. Granite salvaged from the ruins was used for the lower wall of the new. Rising from this wall, a new carved limestone "literal fragment" faithfully reproduces early Norman stonework, recalling the destroyed church. This fragment was modeled by computer for study and presentation, and digital files were provided to the stone fabricator for use in preparing shop drawings.

To double the height of the sanctuary without raising the elevation of the roof, the floor of the church was dropped a level into what was formerly classroom space. The sanctuary end walls are separated from the main roof to allow soft ambient light to wash the unpainted plaster interior surfaces front and rear.

A large concert quality tracker organ was designed to be the center of an active music program. The organ was also modeled and rendered by computer, and digital images were provided to the English Organ Company for fabrication.

Peter L. Gluck and Partners

renderer/partner-in-charge
Kent Larson

Synagogue in Scarsdale

Scarsdale, New York

A rectangular form defines the seating area of this new sanctuary for a growing congregation. Triangular tube-steel trusses, separated by a two-foot-wide skylight zone, frame the ceiling. Fabric panels at the trusses provide acoustical control. The Bema, where the arc is read, is at the precise center of this space, and curved seating is focused on the arc.

Walls enclosing this form open up on two sides to a separate "sacred zone" where the arc and podium are located. This skewed, L-shaped zone is slightly raised, and filled with light from a continuous skylight that links the seating form to the skewed walls. The two canted walls just touch at the lowest point of their meeting, forming a full-height corner window.

Peter L. Gluck and Partners

renderer/partner-in-charge
Kent Larson

Kellner Dileo Office

New York, New York

Critical to Kellner Dileo's operation is the relationship between the president, the research department, and the traders. The president must be able to see and hear what goes on in the trading area and the research department, and be able to communicate directly with both. He must also, at times, have privacy. The researchers and traders must be able to communicate with each other without unduly disturbing the president.

These contradictory requirements were met with the design of sliding glass doors for the president's large office, which enable precise control of the degree of privacy/openness. For staff meetings, the president's office and the trading area become one space. Computer graphics were used to study and present alternative solutions for the planning, lighting, finishes, workstation design, and trading equipment layout.

ESSAYS ON COMPUTER-GENERATED ARCHITECTURAL RENDERINGS

"Technological Achievements in 3D Modeling"
by Mieczyslaw Boryslawski/View by View, Inc.

"Digital Light and Space"
by Kent Larson

"Historiography and Computer Renderings: A Reconstruction of the Josephine Baker House" by Stephen Atkinson

"Cinematic Views of Architecture through Computer Renderings"
by Richard Dubrow/Jon Kletzien /Advanced Media Design

"Hyper-Realism in Architectural Renderings"
by Michael Sechman

Aramco
Dhahran, Saudi Arabia
Skidmore, Owings & Merrill

Technological Achievements in 3D Modeling

Mieczyslaw Boryslawski

In the 20th century, the computer has furthered the development of human beings more than any previous invention. It has helped the design community visualize the unimaginable, consolidate insurmountable data, and bring abstract notions of science into tangible visual images, a step closer to virtual reality. This technology, in light of its capacity to produce informative and powerful images, can expand the designer's visual aptitude and ultimately raise the profession to new heights.

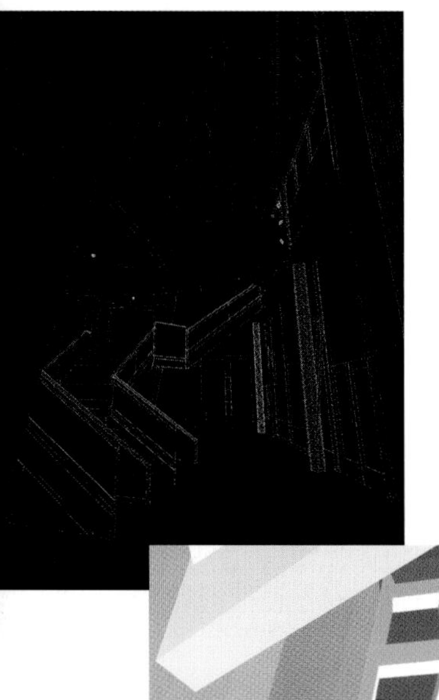

The explosion of hardware and software technology, combined with increased affordability, has created a new digital information explosion, that of 3D computer-based rendering.

3D Models: Purpose and History

Architects make models for many reasons: to study and assess their designs, and to guide the builder in the course of construction. Models are submitted to design competitions in order to win commissions. Whereas study models are a practical tool that architects use to work out design problems, presentation models are intended to impress.

The practice of making models dates back to antiquity. In the second half of the 14th century, models were made especially in connection with the construction of large cathedrals. In the 15th and 16th centuries, models were used in every phase of the architectural design process, from development of initial ideas to the presentation of finished schemes. As Leon Battista Alberti wrote in *On the Art of Building*, in 1486: "I will never tire of recommending the custom, practiced by best architects, of preparing not only drawings and sketches, but also models of wood or other materials. These enable us to examine the work as a whole and, before continuing any further, to estimate the likely trouble and expense."

As the modern world entered the "Information Age," architect Frank Lloyd Wright had a vision of his own. If we substitute the word "computer" for the word "machine," the following statement by Wright is quite relevant today: "The machine can be nowhere creator except as it may be a good tool in the creative artist's toolbox. It is only when you try to make a living thing of the machine itself that you begin to betray your human birthright. The machine can do great work - yes - but only when in the hand of one who knows how to put it to suitable work for the human being."

The use of the computer as a visualization tool puts us on a new frontier. As we begin to publish rather than draw documents we also begin to feel the need for a new level of information service, something more akin to API or UPI or Reuters. Imagine having accumulated knowledge and experience at your fingertips the next time you design a building.

With the 3D visualization technology now available at a reasonable price, all of the parties involved in the design review and approval process can participate interactively and study numerous design iterations within a short time frame. This constant interaction with our clients and their designers is particularly rewarding. It allows the client to participate in "brainstorming" session whereby design decisions are visualized immediately and understood by all the members of the team. "This capability is important because it saves what we have the least of, which is time," says Michael Willis, a San Francisco architect.

3D computer-generated architectural visualization could be divided into two sections: modeling (including scene building) and rendering.

The Modeling Process

A 3D digital model contains geometric data defined in relationship to 3D Cartesian coordinates of X,Y, and Z. Modeling is the creation of 3D geometry, referred to as objects. These

Above: *Three dimensional computer model and rendering presented to the International Olympic Committee as part of Istanbul (Turkey) bid for the Olympics for the year 2000. The complex was designed by Stang & Newdow Architects.* **Opposite Page:** *Wireframe and interior perspectives of the San Jose Repertory Theater Lobby, designed by Holt, Hinshaw Architects. San Francisco, California.*

3D objects are then used to compose a 3D world scene. Digital modeling has a great advantage over the traditional methods used for many years and still in use today. 3D digital models can be changed at any time during the design process at a minimal cost, and they can be interactive. The greatest advantage of 3D digital models over the traditional models is the ability of the viewer to enter the model and view it from the inside, since the digital models are generally built to full scale.

To produce a 3D computer-generated model, it is necessary to understand the designer's vision of the overall design concept. Because of the amount of detail that is so often incorporated into architectural models, the philosophy toward software should be to acquire few programs rather than dabbling in the many on the market. The old adage of "jack of all trades, master of none" is too often the case. There is only one way to get the most out of any software program, and that is by using it on an actual project and getting the job done! 3D computer modeling is the most important stage and a prerequisite to a correctly rendered image. It is not uncommon for a renderer to rely on texture or bump maps instead of spending time creating a detailed model. The more refined the details in the 3D model the more beautiful the final rendered image will be, as every shadow line within the final rendering counts.

Most 3D-modeling applications are generic in nature. They are developed for various modeling tasks such as product advertising, animation, etc. Only a few 3D applications are applicable to architecture. One of the most important features to look for in a 3D architectural application is the layering capabilities. These layers are extremely important in order to separate the objects

that will receive different attributes such as color, texture, lighting, and transparency. These layers should be accessible at all times and located on the desktop as you will use them all the time. You should have as many layers as possible, but the more layers in use, the more housekeeping is required. The problem with many software developers is that they are not the users, and in many cases do not understand the design process. It's impossible to find software that does everything in one application. One should consider investing in an application dealing only with the modeling process, that creates complex models efficiently, and another application that will import these models to be rendered.

Synthetic Rendering Process

Rendering is an image processing technique that takes 3D digital objects or scenes with their assigned physical-based material properties; lighting; and a camera with a chosen field of view in position, and generates a synthetic picture.

The 3D model, besides containing geometric data, may also contain other information regarding material properties of each object and the lighting within the scene. To render a photo-realistic image, more information is needed, such as the object's color, texture, and lighting. For a glass object, a degree of transparency, edge density, and reflections can be applied. This extra information is commonly referred to as specifying object attributes.

Texture Mapping

Assigning a material to an object is similar to the specification provided to the building contractor. In order to duplicate the object's surface quality, it is necessary to obtain this information in a digital format. One way to create a texture map is by scanning a physical sample material provided by the designer or to scan a photograph. A texture may be created within a paint program like Photoshop™. This technique is referred to as texture bitmapping. The surface of the object is based on the bitmap image and looks as if the image was painted onto the object. You can assign bitmaps to change other properties of a material, such as bump maps, specular maps, reflection maps, and opacity maps. In addition to bitmaps, some high-end rendering software provides a procedural method of applying a 3D texture. This texture is written in a computer code language and, once mastered, can be modified. Third-party developers provide libraries of procedural volume shaders or solid shaders. This method provides somewhat better quality of texture since it generates a solid 3D pattern during the rendering process and it does not require mapping coordinates to properly map texture to a complex object.

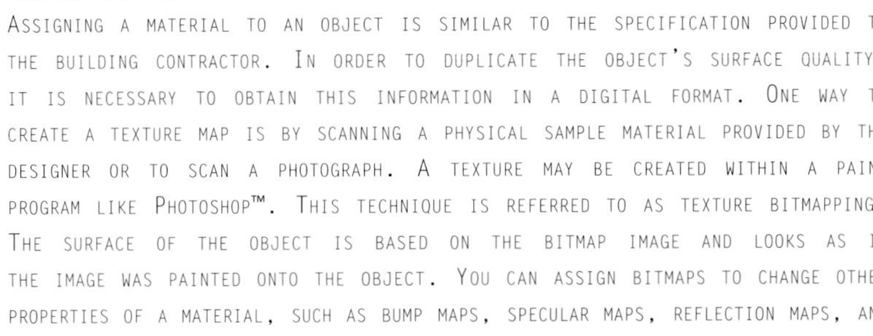

Lighting Objects or Scenes

This process is the most difficult and time consuming as digital light behaves somewhat differently than in an actual situation, and is one of the most challenging and least understood tasks in a synthetic rendering process. There are a variety of types of light sources available to illuminate a scene: spotlights, ambient light, radial lights, parallel lights, tube lights, or camera light. Having studied architectural photography some years ago, I have tried to apply my lighting knowledge to the world of digital lighting. But I soon learned that digital lighting behaves much differently than traditional lighting techniques. The only way to create well-lighted scenes is by trial and error. A parallel light source behaves much like the sun. A low radial light added to a parallel light will lighten the hard shadows, while ambient light will add or subtract to the overall lighting of the scene. In a

complex scene over a hundred light sources of different types could be placed over the site and many tests must be conducted before a final satisfying rendering is produced.

Many architects would argue that the traditional method of hand rendering gives the drawing a human touch, whereas the synthetic rendering tends to look somewhat plastic. This argument has some validity, and it takes an experienced person to produce electronic renderings that will satisfy an experienced traditional renderer. The greatest advantage of electronic rendering is that the digital rendering can be changed relatively painlessly and in a timely manner. Gone are the days of scraping away, cutting, and pasting with paper and pen. The computer is much more forgiving than watercolor paper. Paint in some trees, and if you don't like the way they look, simply "revert" back to the original image. Try doing that with gouache!

In a simple shading rendering technique, only the light coming directly from the source is considered in the shading process. In more realistic and accurate images, it is important not only to take into account the light source itself, but also how all the surfaces and objects in the scene interact with the light. Lighting a 3D scene is a complex and time-consuming process, both in terms of required computing power and the time it takes to place and experiment with light sources. What is more economical: investing in a tool that is fast, accurate, and easy to use but costly, or a tool that is much less expensive but takes more time? I personally find it more rewarding to be able to concentrate on lighting techniques and previewing the rendered image in a matter of seconds or minutes while still concentrating on possible improvement, than waiting for hours for the image to appear. Creating beautiful, true-to-life images is like playing music; one must experiment and practice until satisfied with the results. We all have limits as to the time we can spend on a project in order to compete in this fast-growing marketplace and remain in business. Clients have budgets and once they realize the economic benefits of having high-quality projects produced in digital media, they will be willing to increase their spending. It won't be long before this form of visualization becomes the standard practice within the design profession and a requirement.

Emerging Technologies

New directions are rapidly emerging in modern photometry that promise to revolutionize our understanding of light, hence improving our ability to communicate lighting designs. The wonderful computerized renderings in this book are more than pretty pictures. Some are photometrically accurate representations of real-life situations, such as the cover of this book. There are three converging directions in photometric research: near-field photometry, three-dimensional illuminance, and radiosity. Of these, radiosity is of great importance to an architectural computer renderer.

Radiosity versus Ray Tracing

Radiosity and ray tracing algorithms are very different and yet they are in many ways complementary. Ray tracing is very versatile because of the large range of lighting effects it can model. Radiosity is an advanced form of ray tracing. Images produced using ray tracing techniques tend to look somewhat artificial, with sharp-edged shadows. Although they look realistic, they are not suitable for detailed photometric analysis. Ray tracing a complex model may take hours for a computer to render. It is important to understand the technology of both techniques to achieve the required results.

Previous Spread: *(left page) Existing site condition and 3D computer model of the proposed UCSF/Mount Zion Cancer Center, San Francisco. Designed by Hammel, Green & Abrahamson Architects. (right page) Existing site condition and photomontage showing proposed building and landscape for the Kapiolani / Pikoi Tower, Honolulu, Hawaii.*

This Page: *(above) Yerba Buena Gardens, San Francisco. The development includes the San Francisco Museum of Modern Art by Mario Botta (left); the Center for the Arts Theater by James Stewart Polshek; Visual Arts Building by Fumihiko Maki; Griffin/Related Office Building by Pei Cobb Freed and Partners; Yerba Buena Towers by Cesar Pelli; and the Yerba Buena Esplanade by Michell Giurgola Architects.*

Opposite Page and Following Spread: Existing site condition and 3D rendering photomontage of *Yerba Buena Entertainment/Retail Center by SMWM, / Gary E. Handel Associates.*

Radiance™, an application program developed by the Lawrence Berkeley Laboratory department of day lighting, was originally developed as a research tool for predicting the distribution of visible radiation in illuminated spaces. It uses the technique of ray tracing that follows light backward from the image plane to the source(s). Because it can produce realistic images from a simple description, Radiance™ has a wide range of application in graphic arts, lighting design, and computer-generated architecture. Radiance™ is available free of charge but it has a complex user interface, and is therefore difficult to use.

Lightscape™ is another very powerful application developed by Lightscape Technologies, Inc., of San Jose, CA., and it is the first visualization application based primarily on radiosity techniques. Neither radiosity nor ray tracing offers a total solution for simulating all global illumination effects. Radiosity excels at rendering diffuse-to-diffuse interreflections and ray tracing excels at rendering specular reflections. This post-process radiosity and ray tracing solution offers the best of both worlds. It is possible to combine a ray tracing post-process with a specific view of a radiosity solution to add specular reflections and transparency effects. This radiosity solution replaces the inaccurate ambient constant with accurate indirect illumination value, therefore generating a much more realistic image. Lighscape is probably the most accurate and innovative application today for calculating and rendering accurate lighting simulations of 3D architectural digital models. The application uses a proprietary radiosity technique to calculate direct illumination and indirect diffuse interreflections of light between surfaces. An integrated ray tracer is also provided to add specular highlights and reflections to specific views. All surface materials are defined according to the physical characteristics of diffuse and specular reflectivities. Lightscape calculates all light energy distribution in physical photometric units. There is no limitation to the number of lights which may be included in the scene.

Is Virtual Reality the Future of the Design Profession?

Today we have the technical ability to allow the designer and the client to realistically explore and experience unbuilt projects. This virtual space exploration has its price: low resolution display, chunky headsets, electronic gloves, and very expensive computer systems. The problem and the danger with virtual reality technology is its side effects, such as motion sickness.

Apple Computer's Quick Time VR does not require the elaborate paraphernalia associated with virtual reality. Creating interactive 360-degree panoramic views or walk-throughs in Quick Time VR is quite simple. One can create a walk-through just by combining photographs, computer-rendered images, or both. This innovative technology will allow designers to publish their visions in an interactive CD-ROM format and distribute it to all members of the team. It can be viewed with the standard CD-ROM player found on any computer platform. Apple Computer is currently working with View By View•interactive inc. on the "White House Tour" project. The viewer will be able not only to see a 3D computer-generated fly-by of the White House but once the digital camera takes the viewer into the White House on the tour, the interactive Quick Time VR technology will take over.

Viewing 3D Images in 3D Space

The best and the most natural way to view 3D images is in a 3D space, again without complex head-gear. Currently, 3D computer-rendered images are displayed on computer screens. An innovative technology developed by Dimensional Media Associates may hold a key to unlocking 3D image display capabilities. The High Definition Volumetric Display (HDVD), as it is called, is an advanced, high precision 3D autostereoscopic volume imaging process that functions on the basis of collecting light rays from either single or multiple sources. The system then reassembles and projects the aggregate light rays into a 3D aerial image. The "Real Image" created is brilliant, full color, and appears as a solid object floating in midair that can be viewed in daylight or under controlled lighting conditions. As designers we would be able to sit around a table and view the projected architectural 3D model, rendering, or animation floating on the center of the table or in the palm of your hand. We will be able to interactively change the design in virtual space and in real time without the constraints of 2D monitors. This technology will change the ways we work and interact. The innovative tools are here. All that remains is to embrace them and to put them to use for the good of this planet.

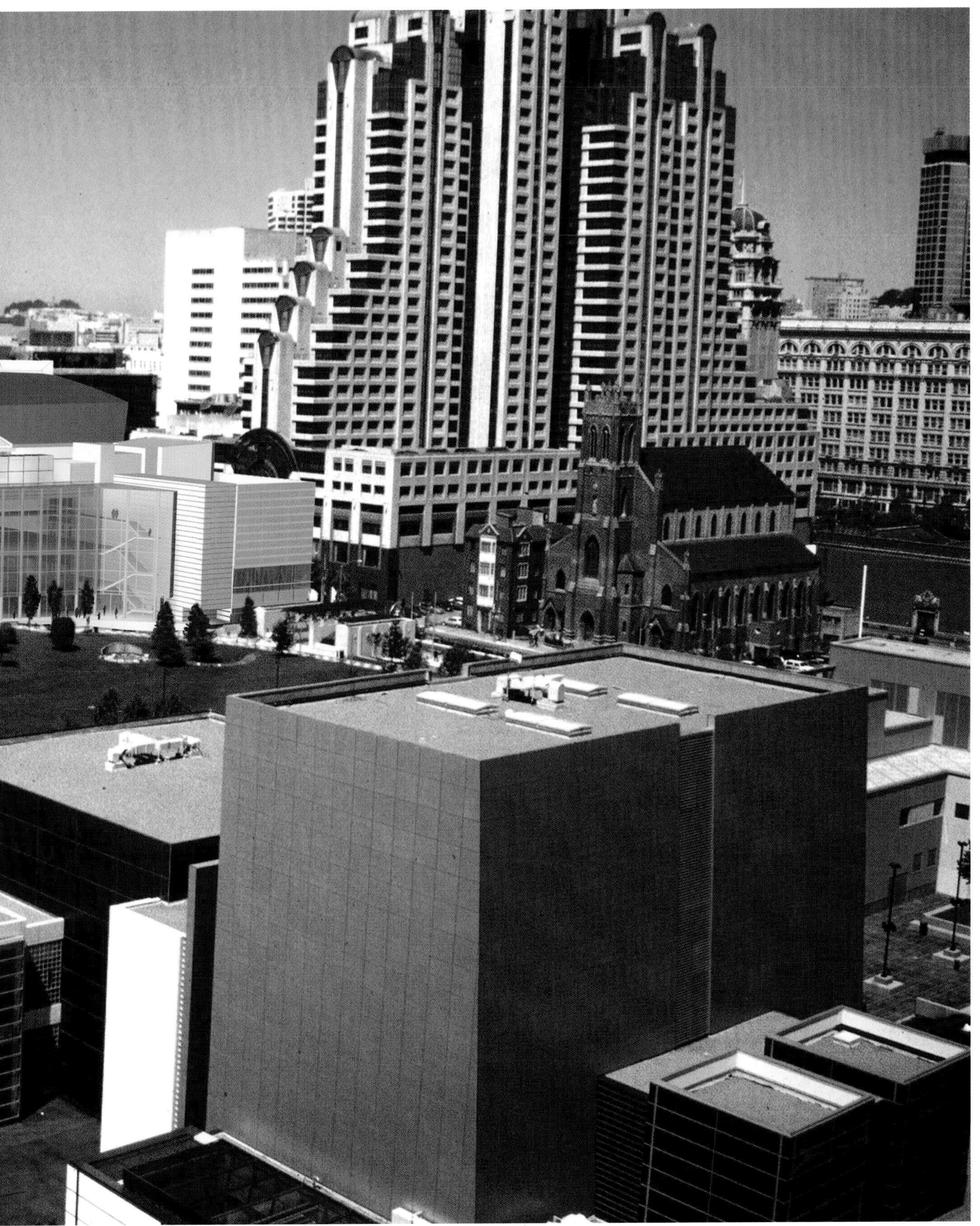

Digital Light and Space

Kent Larson

Architects have long dealt with the poetry of light in space. For evidence of this, one need only watch the moving disc of light transform the interior of the Pantheon. Little of the space is ever directly lit. It is the subtle ambient light in contrast to the intense spot of sun which gives the Pantheon its unique character.

Few of us take the time to observe how extraordinarily complex is the path of light in a naturally lit space. Sunlight hits various surfaces, scattering in directions determined by the angle of incidence and the texture of the material. It bounces off surface after surface until the energy becomes negligible. With each iteration the light picks up something of the color of the material last hit. Surfaces which receive no direct light are brighter or darker depending on their relationship to those that do. This intricate configuration changes hour by hour and season by season, varying dramatically according to haze and cloud conditions.

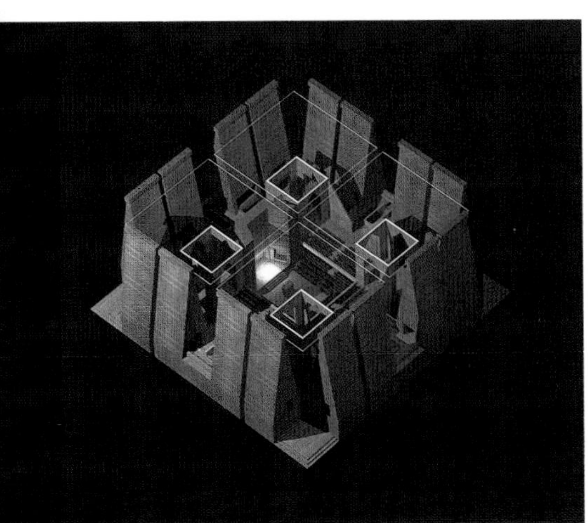

Lighting designers have techniques to predict the behavior of light, but these work best when the variables are small, sunlight is excluded, and the effects of reflected light are ignored. They are not very helpful for light as complex as that of the Pantheon. As each coffer has a unique orientation in space and relationship to the shaft of sunlight, the pattern of shadows and the intensity of the ambient light for each is different, and changes dynamically as the direct light moves. Close up the oculus and hang a few sodium vapor lamps, and a good lighting consultant could more reliably predict the result. Architects who successfully craft daylight have relied primarily on intuition and comparison to past work for the evaluation of complex natural lighting conditions. That the play of natural light has been largely unpredictable is part of its appeal, usually surprising both architect and user with its endless ability to alter the experience of a space. The complexity and dynamism of light makes naturally lit spaces so emotionally satisfying, but this is an illusive, intangible quality, difficult to anticipate.

Louis I. Kahn's unbuilt Hurva synagogue could have been one of the great experiments with the manipulation of sunlight. It was not difficult to settle on this project as one of the first unbuilt spaces to explore using the new digital tools which simulate light. Few architects created space with such power and presence, and this was certainly one of Kahn's most powerful ideas. Few architects were as concerned with light. Kahn's writings are often as difficult and unhelpful as his architecture is clear and direct, but when he speaks of light it is easy to relate his words to his buildings. Just a few examples:

"Light is the giver of all presences"......"Even a space intended to be dark should have enough light from some mysterious opening to tell us how dark it really is. Each space must be defined by its structure and the character of its natural light"......."Natural light gives mood to the space by the nuances of light in the time of day and the seasons of the year, as it enters and modifies the space"......"A room without natural light is not a room"......"All material is spent light."

With Hurva, Kahn had an opportunity to work with the intense light of the desert, rendered so powerfully in his travel sketches of Egypt twenty-five years earlier. By wrapping sixteen massive pylons around an inner sanctuary, and separating the ceiling forms with a cross-shaped skylight, a marvelous pattern of shafts of sunlight strikes the interior.

But Kahn's use of light in Hurva went well beyond just patterns of sunlight, which is only the most obvious feature. He often faced windows toward sunlit exterior walls with openings in order to create a transition from a relatively dark interior to the bright exterior. These "sun walls" would trap light and allow it to bounce between wall

SURFACES. WHEN CONDITIONS ARE RIGHT, A MAGICAL, LUMINOUS, GLOWING SEPARATION BETWEEN INSIDE TO OUT IS CREATED. AS KAHN WROTE:

"I CAME TO THE REALIZATION THAT EVERY WINDOW SHOULD HAVE A FREE WALL TO FACE. THIS WALL, RECEIVING THE LIGHT OF DAY, WOULD HAVE A BOLD OPENING TO THE SKY. THE GLARE IS MODIFIED BY THE LIGHTED WALL, AND THE VIEW IS NOT SHUT OFF. IN THIS WAY, THE CONTRAST MADE BY THE SEPARATED PATTERNS OF GLARE...IS AVOIDED."

WE FIND THIS TECHNIQUE USED TO BEAUTIFUL AND DRAMATIC EFFECT IN HURVA - A RESULT OF PERHAPS KAHN'S CLEAREST APPLICATION AT HURVA OF HIS CONCEPT OF "RUINS WRAPPED AROUND BUILDINGS," WHICH CAN ALSO BE FOUND AT THE SALK INSTITUTE, DHAKA, AND EXETER LIBRARY. HURVA IS COMPOSED OF AN INNER BEIS MIDRASH OR HOUSE OF LEARNING, SURROUNDED BY RUINS. THE INTERIOR IS A SANCTUARY OF CONCRETE AND SHADOWS, PROTECTED AND ENCLOSED BY SIXTEEN MASSIVE PYLONS - PRIMITIVE FORMS BUILT FROM THE SAME LOCAL JERUSALEM STONE AS THE NEARBY WESTERN WALL. LOOKING WEST FROM THE PRECISELY CENTERED ALTER WITH THE SUN IN THE EAST, ONE SEES THE SUNLIT TOPS OF THE PYLONS, WHICH THROW LIGHT ON THE UNSEEN FACING CONCRETE. THE CONCRETE, IN TURN, REFLECTS A SOFT LUMINOUS LIGHT BACK ON THE LOWER PORTION OF THE PYLONS. THROUGH GAPS IN THE SOFTLY ILLUMINATED PYLONS, WE VIEW THE SKY AND THE CITY LIT BY THE INTENSE SUN OF THE DESERT, WHICH MODERATES THE HARSH GLARE WE WOULD OTHERWISE EXPERIENCE. THE SANCTUARY IS LIT BOTH BY THE SLICES OF SUNLIGHT AND THE YELLOW LIGHT FROM THE GLOWING JERUSALEM STONE. THIS INTERMEDIATE ZONE BETWEEN INTERIOR AND EXTERIOR - A FASCINATING SPACE WHERE THE TAPERING PYLONS AND SLOPING CEILING PLANES NEVER QUITE TOUCH - THEREFORE FUNCTIONS AS A LARGE LIGHT DIFFUSER AND FILTER. THE PYLONS ARE BOTH THE SUN WALLS AND THE RUINS OF HURVA.

SHAFTS OF DIRECT LIGHT WHICH ENTER THE INNER SANCTUARY CREATE YET MORE DIFFUSE LIGHT. SUNLIGHT HITS THE FLOOR JUST OUT OF VIEW AT THE BOTTOM OF THE IMAGE ON THE LOWER LEFT. THE BACK OF THE WOOD PEW AT THE BOTTOM CENTER OF THE IMAGE RECEIVES NO DIRECT LIGHT BUT GLOWS BRIGHTLY - LIT BY THE SUNLIGHT REFLECTED FROM THE TRAVERTINE FLOOR. LIKEWISE, THE CONCRETE SURFACE WHICH FACES AWAY FROM THE SUN IS BRIGHTLY LIT ONLY FROM THIS REFLECTED LIGHT. SINCE THIS INDIRECT SOURCE IS A RECTANGLE OF LIGHT ON THE FLOOR, THE SHADOWS CAST UPWARD ON THE CONCRETE WALL HAVE SOFT EDGES IN CONTRAST TO THE DISTINCT BOUNDARIES OF THOSE CAST FROM THE SUN - A POINT SOURCE.

WHEREAS HURVA HAS ONE SINGLE INTENSE DRAMATIC SOURCE OF LIGHT - THE SUN - UNITY TEMPLE HAS TRANSLUCENT SKYLIGHTS, WINDOWS, AND SPHERES OF INCANDESCENT LIGHT WHICH SOFTLY ILLUMINATE THE SPACE AND CREATE VERY SUBTLE PATTERNS OF AMBIENT LIGHT AND SHADOWS. THE MULTIPLE AREA LIGHTS (LIGHT SOURCES THAT ARE LARGER THAN A POINT SOURCE) CREATE OVERLAPPING SHADOW PATTERNS WITH NO DISTINCT EDGES, WHICH CAN BE CLEARLY SEEN ON THE FLOOR BENEATH THE PEWS. WRIGHT'S BUILDING HAS PRIMARILY PAINTED SURFACES WITH SOFT COLORS, NOT THE RICH TEXTURE OF CONCRETE, STONE, AND ASH FOUND IN HURVA. THE SOFT GRADATIONS OF LIGHT AND DARK ON PAINTED SURFACES GIVE THE SPACE ITS TEXTURE.

KAHN IN HIS DAY USED WHAT WAS PROBABLY THE BEST TOOL AVAILABLE FOR VISUALIZING LIGHT: LARGE INTERIOR STUDY MODELS LIT BY INCANDESCENT LAMPS TO SIMULATE THE SUN. THAT THIS WORKED FOR HIM THERE CAN BE NO DOUBT, BUT A REVIEW OF THE MODEL PHOTOGRAPHS MADE BY KAHN'S OFFICE REVEAL THAT QUITE A LEAP OF THE IMAGINATION IS REQUIRED TO UNDERSTAND WHAT WOULD REALLY HAPPEN WITH LIGHT IN THE FINISHED SPACE. THE MODELS ARE SCHEMATIC AND LACK DETAIL AND A DELINEATION OF MATERIALS. THE LIGHT, IN MOST CASES, ONLY BEGINS TO APPROXIMATE WHAT WOULD HAVE OCCURRED IN THE BUILT

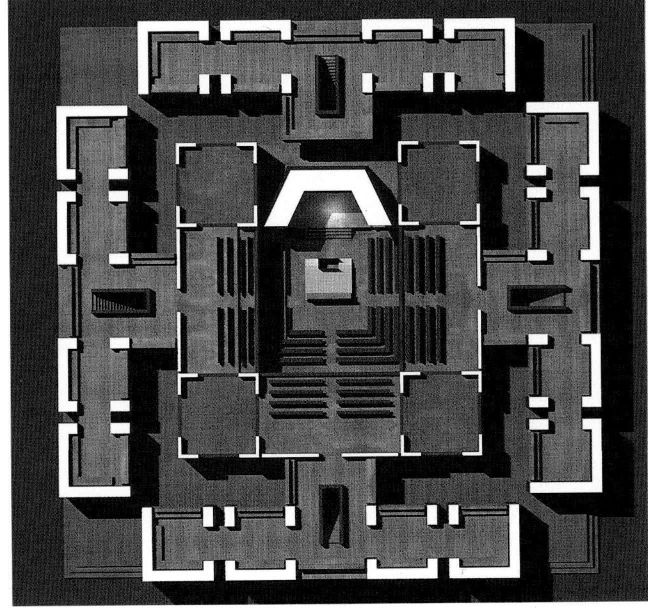

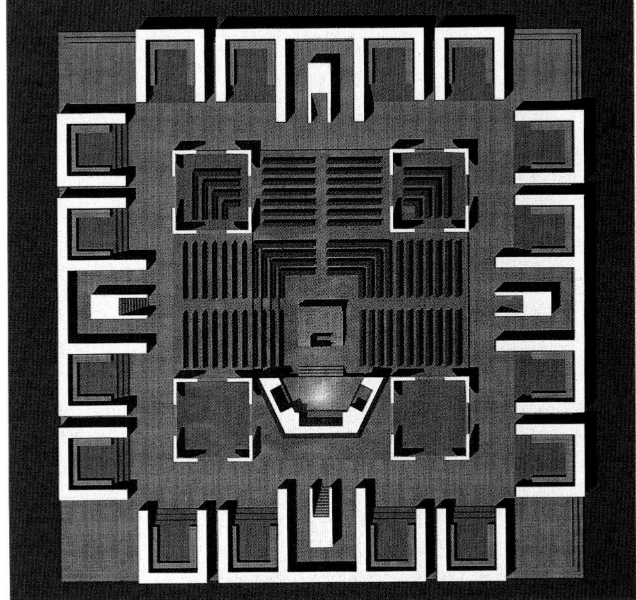

SPACE, AS IS EVIDENT IN A COMPARISON TO PHOTOGRAPHS OF THE COMPLETED PROJECT. WRIGHT, A SUPREMELY TALENTED DRAFTSMAN, STUDIED AND PRESENTED SPACE GRAPHICALLY. IF HIS WONDERFUL PENCIL AND WATERCOLOR DRAWINGS DID NOT ACTUALLY DEPICT LIGHT AS A CAMERA WOULD CAPTURE IT, THEY WERE NONETHELESS QUITE EFFECTIVE AT COMMUNICATING HOW THE BUILDING WOULD BE EXPERIENCED.

TODAY WE HAVE THE TOOLS TO VERY ACCURATELY APPROXIMATE THE COMPLEX PLAY OF LIGHT AND MATERIALS IN SPACE. WE CAN CREATE DIGITAL IMAGES WHICH ARE CAPABLE OF REFLECTING REALITY AS ACCURATELY AS A PHOTOGRAPH. BUT WHAT DOES THIS REALLY MEAN?

A PHOTOGRAPHER WILL CLAIM THAT PHOTOGRAPHIC TOOLS ARE USED TO CAPTURE A VERY PERSONAL IMPRESSION OF WHAT IS IN FRONT OF THE CAMERA. THE REALITY RECORDED IS ALWAYS FILTERED BY THE SENSITIVITIES OF AN ARTIST. ON THE OTHER HAND, DEVELOPERS OF DIGITAL LIGHTING SIMULATION TOOLS WILL TELL YOU THAT THE GOAL IS TO ENABLE THE PRODUCTION OF PHYSICALLY ACCURATE SIMULATIONS OF LIGHT AND MATERIALS IN SPACE - IMAGES WHICH ARE AS TRUE A REPRESENTATION OF REALITY AS IS A PHOTOGRAPH. THEY MAY ACTUALLY BRISTLE AT THE SUGGESTION THAT THEIR SOFTWARE IS "JUST" A RENDERING TOOL TO BE USED WITH ARTISTIC LICENSE.

BUT THE PHOTOGRAPHIC IMAGE IS AFFECTED BY A WHOLE RANGE OF VARIABLES BEGINNING, FUNDAMENTALLY, WITH WHO IS BEHIND THE CAMERA, THE SELECTION OF FILM, THE LENS, AND THE APERTURE SETTING. PRIOR TO DIGITAL PHOTOGRAPHY, THE PROCESSING CHEMISTRY, AGITATION, CORRECTION FILTERS, PRINTING PAPER, AND DODGE AND BURN TECHNIQUE GREATLY EFFECTED THE RESULTS. EVEN IF MY FOUR-YEAR-OLD HAPPENED TO AIM HER LITTLE OLYMPUS AT EXACTLY THE SAME POINT IN SPACE AND TIME AS A STEIGLITZ, THERE IS LITTLE CHANCE THEY WOULD END UP WITH THE SAME IMAGE.

MOST PHOTOGRAPHS PUBLISHED TODAY ARE DIGITALLY EDITED AND ENHANCED - BODIES ARE MADE FLAWLESS, IRRELEVANT DETAIL AND PEOPLE ARE DELETED, AND MEANING AND MOODS ARE MANIPULATED ALL IN THE INTEREST OF MARKET SHARE (AS WITH O.J.'S ARTIFICIALLY INDUCED, THUG-LIKE FIVE O'CLOCK SHADOW). SOME IN JOURNALISM HAVE PROPOSED AN INTERNATIONAL SYMBOL TO FLAG A DIGITALLY DOCTORED IMAGE, BUT ITS STRICT APPLICATION WOULD RESULT IN SUCH WIDESPREAD USE THAT IT WOULD SOON BE RENDERED MEANINGLESS. EVEN IF A PRINTED IMAGE IS NOT DOCTORED AND ACCURATELY REFLECTS WHAT THE PHOTOGRAPHER'S EYE SAW AT THAT MOMENT, IT DOES NOT NECESSARILY REFLECT REALITY. AN ARCHITECTURAL PHOTOGRAPHER WILL BRING CASES OF FILL LIGHTS TO AN ASSIGNMENT TO ALTER, SOMETIMES DRAMATICALLY, THE LIGHT IN A SPACE IN PURSUIT OF A MORE PERFECT IMAGE. THE PRINTED IMAGE IN A MAGAZINE MAY BE CLOSER TO WHAT AN ARCHITECT WOULD PREFER, BUT QUITE DIFFERENT FROM WHAT A USER EXPERIENCES.

ALL OF THIS IS ONLY TO SAY THAT THE TERM PHOTO-REALISM HAS BECOME A MEANINGLESS EXPRESSION. GOING BACK A DIGITAL GENERATION TO, SAY, 1992, IT WAS ENOUGH TO SHOW A LITTLE WOOD GRAIN AND REFLECTIONS TO QUALIFY A DIGITAL IMAGE AS PHOTO-REALISTIC, EVEN IF IT WAS FLAT, SYNTHETIC, AND BORE LITTLE RESEMBLANCE TO AN ACTUAL PHOTO. TODAY WE CAN CREATE STARTLINGLY DIFFERENT DIGITAL IMAGES OF THE SAME SPACE, ALL OF WHICH CAN BE MADE TO BE AS CONVINCINGLY "REAL" AS A PHOTOGRAPH. HYPER-REALISM, OR ENHANCED-REALISM, IS REALLY WHAT WE ARE WORKING WITH.

WHAT IS MOST FASCINATING ABOUT THE NEW DIGITAL LIGHTING SIMULATION TOOLS (INTEGRA FOR THE HURVA IMAGES AND LIGHTSCAPE FOR THE UNITY TEMPLE IMAGES) IS THAT THEY ARE FLEXIBLE ENOUGH TO BE USED IN VERY DIFFERENT WAYS ACCORDING TO THE INTEREST AND SKILLS OF THE USER. FOR A LIGHTING DESIGNER, THEY CAN BE USED TO PRECISELY DEFINE THE PROPERTIES OF LIGHTS, DOWN TO THE GONIOMETRIC DIAGRAM AND MAINTENANCE FACTOR OF A PARTICULAR FIXTURE, AND PERFORM THE MILLIONS OF CALCULATIONS REQUIRED TO BOUNCE LIGHT AROUND A SPACE AND CREATE A MAP OF THE AMBIENT LIGHT ILLUMINATING SURFACES. THE FOOTCANDLE READING OF ANY POINT ON

A three-dimensional surface can be queried. In this sense they are objective analytical tools. Alternatively, they can be used artistically to create a subjective impression of a light-filled space. The effects of light dispersion can be amplified, colors can be made more saturated or subdued, contrast can be boosted, shadows can be exaggerated. We can apply as a texture any image we can photograph or create with an image synthesizer. Separate images can be composited to any effect desired. In other words, we can simulate the physical properties of light and materials with much the same accuracy as a lens and film, and we can manipulate them as desired like a photographer in a darkroom. The range of manipulation possibilities, however, is much greater when working digital. With computer graphic imaging we can look through an inconveniently placed wall, adjust the sun, boost or lessen the reflectivity of a surface, or replace a sky.

Returning to Hurva, we will never know how this building would have been completed. Details such as railings, floor finishes, and concrete ties were not delineated and had to be assumed based on contemporary projects. Kahn avoided addressing the difficult problem of how to glaze the space, and it is anyone's guess how this would have been solved had the project been built. The light in this space would have been altered by the properties of the glazing materials used, and no doubt by major revisions to the design as it was refined and problems were resolved.

As a result, this was less an exercise to create a physically accurate simulation, than an attempt to capture something of the essence of the project - to communicate the raw emotional power of the space - to create digital impressions of a building that will never exist.

Stephen Atkinson

Historiography and Computer Renderings: A Reconstruction of the Josephine Baker House

Due to the availability of powerful yet easily accessible image manipulation programs, computers are shaping the direction of much historical research in architecture. There has been a capacity for the rigorous investigation of historical buildings' formal design through image manipulation and rendering. These investigations can fall into many categories: manipulation of photos to show design intentions; reconstructions of unbuilt or altered buildings; conceptual computer imaging as a diagramming tool; exploratory modeling to reveal spatial sequences; massing; and comparisons of different works by the same or different architects.

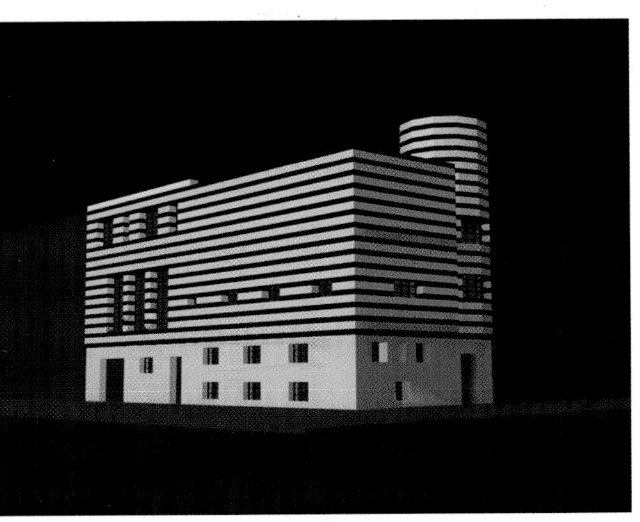

In hyper-realistic reconstructions of unbuilt architecture (where computer images or animations represent the building for the first time in ways comparable to how the actual building would have appeared) the distinction between the original work and its intermediary representation is blurred.

Computer reconstructions, modifications, and suppositions can give profound insight into an architecture which has long since vanished, been irreparably altered, or never built. They may effectively add to an architect's oeuvre, show original intentions, or alter existing assumptions. Furthermore, given the trajectory of computer simulations, it is conceivable that walk-throughs will eventually become so authentic that the term "unbuilt" for these projects seems no longer appropriate as the term really means inexperienced or unrealized. These developments pose great questions and opportunities for architectural historians.

Adolf Loos' unbuilt design for a house for Josephine Baker in Paris revolves around a skylighted swimming pool that has passages and windows that would allow the underwater viewing, ostensibly, of Josephine Baker swimming. The myriad of insightful readings afforded the building is a result as much from the magnificently potent issues it raises regarding space and gender as from the mystery of its inception. Until now, our knowledge of the project was based on historical descriptions in conjunction with orthogonal drawings and an exterior model photo.

The following computer images are to serve as an accurate (though greatly abstracted) portrayal of the interior sequence and light quality. The fiction, as a grounding vehicle for the images.

It was bright and clear that morning, I distinctly recall, when I made my way toward Josephine's to keep a breakfast appointment. Reflecting on the evening's performance, I wondered if she would not be a bit sluggish. Pausing across from the object of my design I considered it a worthy container for a magnificent and exotic presence such as herself. How magnificently it rested amidst the dowdy, overly-embellished mastodons surrounding it. I crossed the street and entered.

I reflected on what Josephine's mood must be the morning after a performance. But I don't believe I've even seen Josephine by day. "Synonymous with the night," I've always said. Gesturing down the narrow hallway, Housekeeper informed me that Josephine would join me shortly in the breakfast room. I moved toward the hall but paused briefly, considering the passage through which I must then pass. How intimate it should be in the quiet of the morning without crowds from a gathering milling about. But the deafening quiet throughout the whole house this morning was itself a bit unsettling - so domestic. Ah...the passage seems to be moving. What...and I moved slowly forward toward the shimmering light. My God she must be swimming...and at this hour. A bit surprised, I slowly inched forward to peer around the edge of the window. And there silhouetted by the cascading light moved Josephine, gracefully and fluidly. So beautiful she was floating there, and in her full nakedness I now saw. Desire gripped me forcefully at that moment in a way that her reviews never had. Indeed I am quite sure that what surprised me most at that time was that her movements were not ones of performance but self-reflection. So personal seemed this moment that at once I felt, not the received

guest, but the voyeur. Whether it was moments or hours that I stood there, my knees weak and my knuckles clutching the sill, watching her glide back and forth, I do not know to this day. But of one thing I am certain, though it was never discussed, neither at the breakfast following, nor anytime thereafter; at some point during this encounter, possession of the hotel was unquestionably and irrevocably transferred to Josephine.

Legend

1. Entry
2. Services
3. Salon
4. Pool
5. Small Salon
6. Cafe
7. Office
8. Bath
9. Bedroom
10. Dining Room

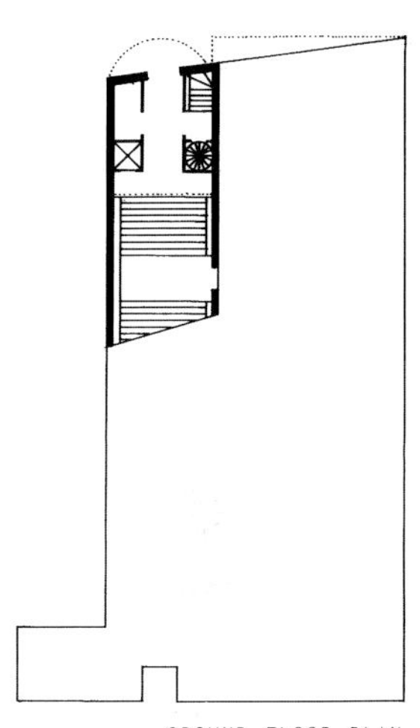
Ground Floor Plan

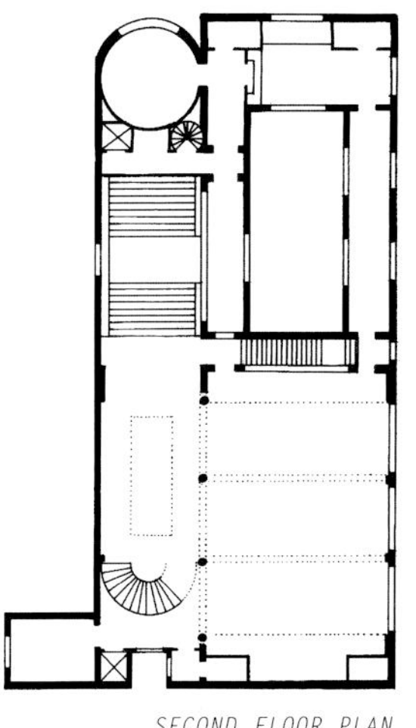
Second Floor Plan

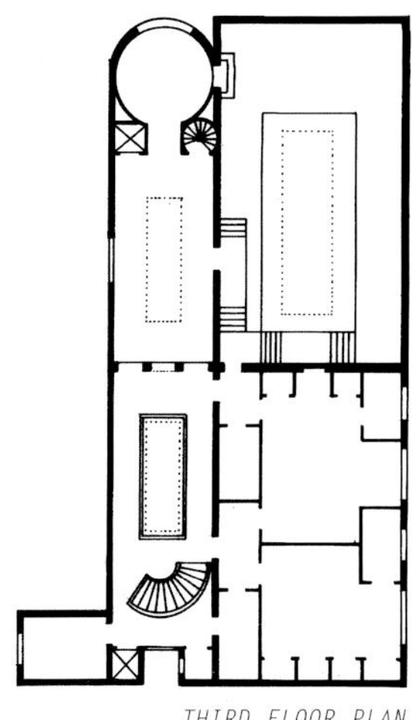
Third Floor Plan

Richard Dubrow/Jon Kletzien

Cinematic Views of Architecture Through Computer Renderings

Computer aided design and its sibling, realistic illustration and animation, have come a long way in the last few years. The advent of high performance, low-cost hardware, in association with accelerated 3D software, have started to transform how we view and present architecture in this digital age. These advances in microprocessor and software codes, however, remain foreign to our senses. The most important influence they have on us is how we relate to and use our computer components, most notably the monitor. In turn, the monitor has given us the opportunity to relate our illustration to the sensibilities of today's world.

The original CAD software products conceived of the monitor as a surrogate drafting table. The monitor's screen replaced a sheet of paper. The mouse or pen stylus replaced ink and pencil. Eraser, T-square, and other drafting tools were contained in the software.

When computer hardware and software became powerful enough to create 3D geometry, and to view this geometry from any angle, the monitor evolved into a much more sophisticated instrument. It became a camera lens through which to view architecture. With this new powerful tool, the influence on representation has become substantial.

Modern expectation of space is moving away from the orders of nature upon which classical illustration methods are based, and toward today's massive entertainment industry. We can no longer look at the convention of plan, section, elevation, and perspective for insight into how to use these new tools of representation. We must look toward the precedents of Hollywood and the great film directors of the last 60 years. The perceptive orders these people have created dominate the modern world and its expectation of our work. The computer monitor is the window through which we relate our work to the world as it has been shaped by film and how we, in turn, perceive it.

The mythical Hollywood portrayal of the director, a camera lens in hand, viewing the set from every conceivable angle to locate the perfect shot, is how we should work, how we as renderers should think. The computer is your "film crew." The 3D model is the "set." The aspects of the design the architect wishes to convey is the "script." The presentation is the "movie." The client is the "audience." The architecture is the "star."

Today's sophisticated design and illustration software packages contain all the tools used by the great directors of Hollywood. Orson Wells and Alfred Hitchcock had no more resources at their disposal, probably even less, than what today's 486-PC or Macintosh desktop computer offer. What they did have was a complete understanding of the orders of these tools and how their thoughtful use influenced the response of the audience. Camera lens size, motion, dolly, roll, and editing, used in combination not only document the space but evoke emotional responses from the viewer.

Stanley Kubrick's *The Shining* offers a clear example of how film directors show architectural space as well as convey the emotional impact of the space. Within this movie, a series of scenes are centered on moving through the hotel hallways. These hallways do not represent any special achievement in architecture. This is a bland space with white walls, a carpeted floor, and the wood doors of hotel rooms. Everyone has been in hallways similar to these; most office buildings or hotels have a similar space. However, in the hands of Kubrick, these are the halls of hell. By manipulating camera height, speed, and lens size, each turn around a corner is an angst-filled moment of emotional pain. How did he squeeze so much from such a bland space? Why did millions of people fall out of the seats just from moving through this hallway?

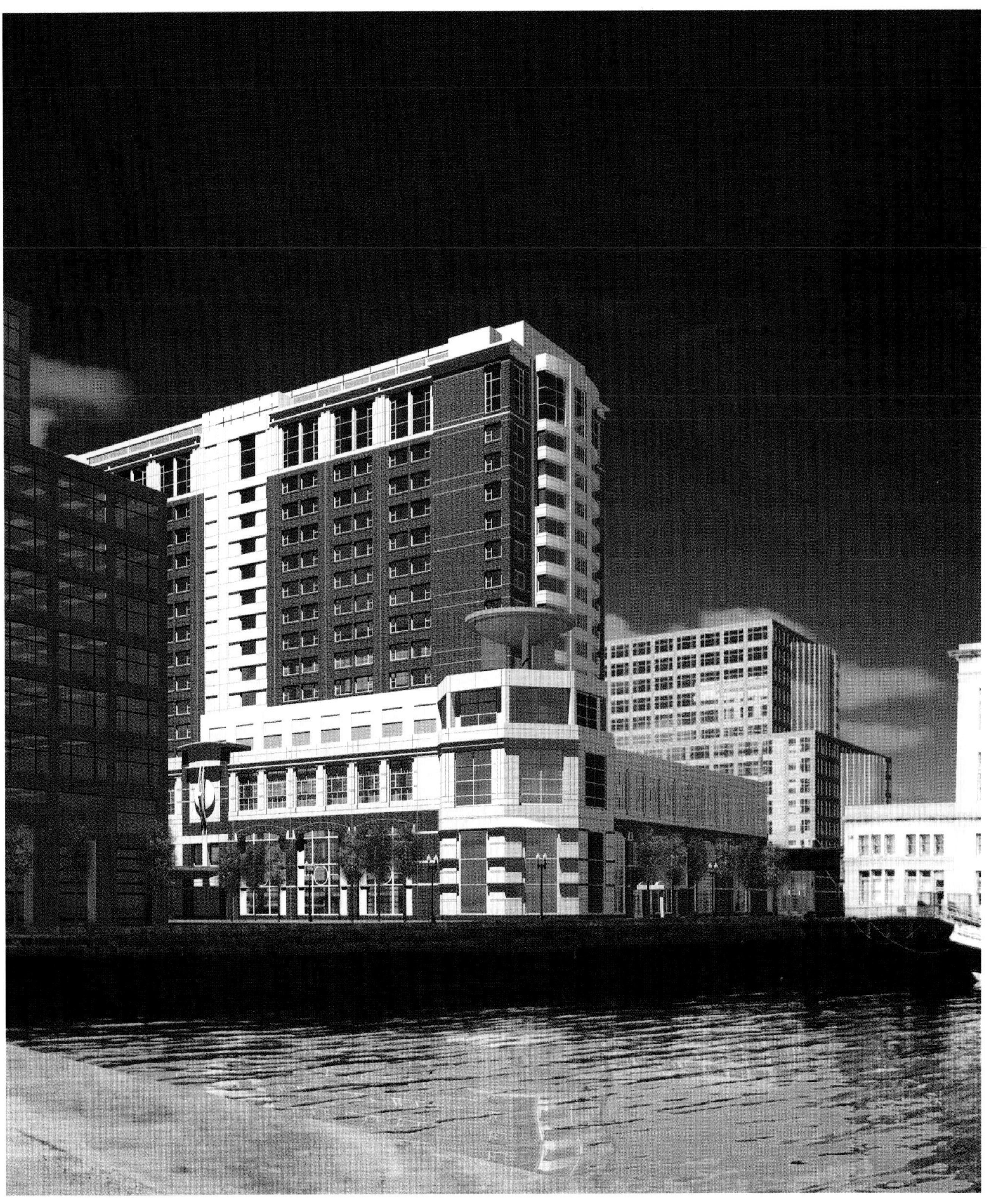

Above: *Photo composite of the hotel at The World Trade Center. A complex Design by The Stubbins Associates architects, Cambridge, Massachusetts. Renderings of the project applying different materials were produced by Advanced Media Design, Providence, Rhode Island.*
Opposite Page: *General view and entrance court of the Shanghai Business Center designed by Pei Cobb Freed and Partners architects. Both renderings are computer/hand composite, produced by Advanced Media Design with Paul Stevenson Oles, FAIA.*

Kubrick used three camera tools to create this scene. First he starts with camera height. Throughout this segment we follow a child riding a Bigwheel through the halls. The camera is placed at the child's head height, very low to the ground. We feel uncomfortably small and somewhat helpless. Next is camera motion, following the child's erratic ride. We move from side to side as well as speeding up and slowing down. This erratic camera motion makes us feel uneasy and nervous, lacking control. Finally, there is the power of the camera lens. Shots down the straight corridor use a small lens size, accentuating the length of the hall. As we round a corner our peripheral vision is limited, allowing anybody hiding around the corner to stay unnoticed until the last possible second.

Could Kubrick use these tools to make this same hallway feel like the safest, most comforting hallway in the whole world? Absolutely! By manipulating his tools, he can evoke any emotional response he wishes. Our community has much to absorb from these entertainment based precedents. Without turning our backs on the rich history of architectural representation, we have begun to incorporate these new tools and techniques. The computer monitor, the potential of its capabilities, is changing the way we work. With this inexpensive piece of equipment, the synthesis of architectural and film sensibility has begun. Through this synthesis, architectural representation is now defining itself within the boundaries of modern expectation.

Hyperrealism in Architectural Renderings

Michael Sechman

Hyperrealism in architectural rendering is the production of highly realistic and quasi-surrealistic images of architecture with the aid of computers, photography and specialized software. The images are surrealistic in the sense that the images transcend realistic scenes because they are not hindered by the constraints of reality. Hyperrealistic architectural renderings use spatial definitions and reality as an armature for the imagination to build upon. Upon this armature, which is often a CAD model, all the power and potential of a computer system can be applied. An understanding of the evolution of the mind-hand creation to the mind-machine creation is of particular importance in understanding the significance of hyperrealism and digital imaging. The allure of computer-created images often leads many to believe that the stunning effects created on computers are primarily the product of the technology. It is this new technology coupled with traditional means of creation that enable the digital artist to produce such outstanding images. Also important is the education and background one brings to any creative process. The greater the understanding of space and light and traditional rendering techniques, the greater the potential of creating a desired intent. What the schools with advanced technology have in store for future students leads one to believe that the digital media will become as commonplace as pencil and paper, and will eventually supplant them.

The history of representational media is one of great leaps over large periods – from the first glyph carvings in stone and cave paintings, to abstract representations of type on paper, to the first printing presses. We are now at the beginning of another great leap. We are only at the beginning of the first wave of what will be known of as the digital epoch. The amount of change and the acceleration of change is daunting, but advances in software and hardware design will soften the learning curve. The combination of better software, faster and less expensive hardware, and the connectivity of systems such as the Internet seems a manifestation of our creations in the image of ourselves. As we are created, so we create. It is the power to create a world to fit the creator's desired image that is so seductive. It is also the ability to more easily include the media of time and sound in animations that makes our creations more attractive. We as a species are particularly sensitive to movement and visual action. The success of television is the most demonstrable example of this. As this technology advances, the distinction between large advances in ability is becoming smaller and smaller. We seem to be accelerating toward innovation with fewer lags between breakthroughs.

The position of the computer graphics user as a creator in a new realm is an apt metaphor. The realization of the creator's dreams and intents is closer at hand with the use of computers and software. In hyperrealistic architectural renderings the scenes elicit these perceptions by the use of photography or procedural techniques. Photography is a two-dimensional rendering of real space and time. In photography one possesses the essences of life. Images created with materials that are not photographically based often are "computer-like"; they are devoid of life-like qualities that are often taken for granted. It is the capture of that life-like quality that is most alluring. A wall in a room has subtle changes in light and texture that are difficult to express well in a computer-created image. Special rendering capabilities such as ray tracing and radiosity are expensive in rendering time. They will be less so in the future, but the wealth of information in photographs is difficult to ignore.

I believe that the use of photography in hyperrealistic renderings is the essential ingredient in producing a life-like perception of reality. The creator designs or receives designs and produces a digital database representing the design. Specifications are given for lighting, materials, and finishes. Materials are scanned and manipulated. The manipulation of the scanned material is critical for the seamless combination of disparate materials captured in different conditions. It is here, in the manipulation of the scanned real world, that the creator's knowledge and experiences in seeing the real world elevates what could have been a photo and paste session to the creation of new worlds. As the future unfolds, procedural processes that emulate (and can go beyond) the abilities of photography will be a critical part of computer rendering.

The use of computer renderings in architecture has only become practical in the last several years. With the use of computers becoming almost mandatory in higher education, the computer has become a ubiquitous tool among many others. The architectural renderer who desires to use computers as a medium for expression must master the language of the software and the many types of hardware combinations necessary for output. Typically, computer renderings require large amounts of memory. It is not unusual for image files to be 40 to 60 megabytes in size. A thorough comprehension of the software packages required to produce architectural renderings is another of the key items fundamental to the process. One must know the abilities and limitations of the systems used, and work around them.

Computers are fascinating because they enable us to create dreams. The visions that are conjured by the mind are fleeting and difficult to express. It seems to me that there will be no practical limits in the realm of creation in computer rendering. The only limitation will be one's dreams and potential for imagination. With immediate global communication possible, one's ability to see the creations of others will only allow further exploration in creativity.

Since the first humans, the desire to express and create has been passionate. The passion of creativity is only heightened with new tools, those that allow us to sense our creations, and enhance the link of the mind-creation process. Computers allow the creator to simulate in theory what would have been impossible only years ago. The abilities and uses of computers are constantly widening. What ultimate future for humankind might be sooner glimpsed with the further vision of these new mediums? Whatever our ultimate fate, we are on the brink of a new expressionism - a digital genesis.

Technical Information

Kohn Pedersen Fox Associates PC

Hardware: IBM-compatible 486 and Pentium desktop computers with Logitech mice are used for construction of the projects in two and three dimensions in CAD. Renderings produced on both Pentium 60 and 90 machines with 16 and 32 MB of RAM and flat 21-inch color monitors. Image adjustment and collaging done on a Pentium 120 machine with 32MB of RAM and a 21-inch flat screen monitor. Typical final image size is between 12 and 22 MB.
Software: For 3-D model construction and 2-D drawing, Microstation Version 5. For rendering, Spotlight Raytracer and Modelview. For Image Adjustment, Adobe PhotoShop version 2.5. and 3.0 for Windows, and Macintosh Desktop Publishing Layout, Quark Express, and Corel Draw.
Output Device: Output of the images is through Xerox electrostatic plotter for large format, HP laser printer for 11x17-inch, and color imaging and slides are handled through outside local service bureaus.

Notes: All software is operated under MS-DOS and Microsoft Windows version 3.1. This platform was chosen for its wide range of applications: using the same computers we are able to generate 2-D drawings, 3-D models and renderings, correspondence, and project management spreadsheets.
KPF is now in the process of computerizing the entire office. Every studio workstation, office, and conference room will be wired for networking, printing, scanning e-mail (internal and external), and data transfer. The network can also be used for distributed processing of renderings throughout the system.

Rafael Viñoly Architects

Hardware: Indigo XS24, Personal Iris, Macintosh Quadra 700 and Power PC500, 386 + 486 PCs running MS-DOS and Microsoft Windows version 3.1, Irix 405, Apple Macintosh running Mac OS.
Software: Alias, Photoshop, AutoCAD Release 12 (Drawings), Alias 4.1 (Modeling and Rendering), Adobe PhotoShop 3.0 (Photo retouching).
Input Device: Video, Digital D1, Nokon Coolscan (Scanning Slides).
Output Device: Iris Print (High-End Color), Canon Fiery (Low-End Color), Digital D1/Beta/One-Inch (Video).

Notes: Plans, sections, and elevations were executed on Silicon Graphics workstations and 386 + 486 Personal Computers using AutoCAD Release 12. Computer Models and renderings were produced on Silicon Graphics stations. Image retouching and correcting was done on Apple Macintosh computers.

Cesar Pelli & Associates

Hardware: IBM-compatible 386, 486, and Pentium desktop computers with SummaSketch tablets used to construct the projects in 3D in CAD. Renderings produced on both Pentium 60 and Pentium 90 machines with 6 to 32 MB of RAM and NEC MultiSync 5FGe 17-inch monitors. Image adjustment and collaging done on a Pentium 60 machine with 32 MB of RAM and a MultiSync 5FGp 17-inch monitor. Typical final image file size was between 12 and 22 MB.
Software: AutoCAD release 12 for DOS (Model Construction), AccuRender version 1 & 2 (Rendering), Adobe PhotoShop version 2.5 & 3.0 for Windows, Kai's Power Tools (Image Adjustment).
Input Device: All scanning was done by a local service bureau.
Output Device: Output of the images was also handled by local service bureaus in two ways, depending on how we wanted to present: Fujix Pictography produces very high resolution, small images that allow very accurate control over color; LazerMaster DisplayMaker digital large format ink jet produces 36-inch output used for presentation.

Notes: All software operated under MS-DOS and Microsoft Windows version 3.1. This platform was chosen by the office for the combination of cost effectiveness and wide range of available applications. The same computers are used to generate 2-D drawings, 3-D renderings, client correspondence, and project management spreadsheets. On average, processing time with the AccuRender software was between three to eight hours to produce a 9 x 12-inch image at 200 dpi. Several more hours were usually spent using PhotoShop to adjust the colors, collage in sky, and repair errors in the model.

Machado & Silvetti Associates

Hardware: Silicon Graphics Personal Iris, Sun Workstations.
Software: Artisan, Adobe Photoshop.
Input Device: Flatbed scanner for trees, sculpture (entitled "Victory"); Slide scanner for brick from Cranbrook campus.
Output Device: Dye-sublimation printer.

Notes: Stone textures were created using Artisan program on Sun workstations and then imported as texture maps. Grass texture was created using a default fractal pattern texture-mapped onto undulating surfaces. Final images were touched up using Artisan and Adobe PhotoShop. Brick textures were created from texture-mapped brick patterns from photographs from the Cranbrook campus arranged on Artisan. Trees were texture-mapped from scanned photos onto flat panels in the computer model. These in turn were oriented toward the viewer in the respective views. Rendering time varied between 4 and 24 hours.

Estudio Becker-Ferrari

Hardware: IBM-compatible 486-66MHz, 24 MB of RAM; Mitsubishi Diamond Scan Monitor; Hewlett Packard Scanjet-c Scanner was used for scanning the background images; Hewlett Packard Laserjet IIIP for printing tests; Tektronix with dye sublimation technology, Summasketch Microgrid II 12x18 as input device.
Software: AutoCAD R12 for DOS, Rendering, Accurender 1.1 (Modeling), Aldus PhotoStyler (Image Edition).

Notes: The daylight images processing time was between 4 and 10 hours to produce 2048 x 1536 pixel images. Nightime images took about 30 hours because of the increasing number of lights. Postprocessing images with PhotoStyler took about 2 hours each.

Office dA

Hardware: DOS Platform, 486 DX2 66 MHz by Compudyne, 300 MB Hard Drive, 32 MB of RAM, SyQuest Removable Drive.
Software: Adobe PhotoShop 2.5.1, AutoCAD Release 12 from AutoDesk for modeling, 3D Studio Release 4 from AutoDesk, Animator Pro from AutoDesk.

Skidmore, Owings & Merrill

Hardware: IBM RS/6000 workstations (3D modeling); 486 and Pentium PC workstations; PowerMacs.
Software: IBM A&ES Model program running AIX and Xwindows (3D modeling/shading); Microstation V5.0; Intergraph Modelview 3.1.0, Strata SudioPro 1.3.2; Micrografx Picture Publisher 4.0 and Adobe Photoshop 3.0 (post-processing)
Input Device: Various materials and background and foreground objects are scanned on HP Color ScanJet and incorporated in the images.

Output Device: The shading images are saved as vector files and plotted directly from in-house Versatec electrostatic color plotters. The rendered images, on the other hand, are most often saved in TIF, Targa or encapsulated Postscript formats and then sent to service bureaus to have IRIS plots or slides made for highest quality. These images could also be plotted from in-house Canon 550/Fiery color copier up to 11" x 17" size.

Gwathmey Siegel & Associates

Hardware: IBM-compatible 486/66 and Pentium 60-based PC. RAM-16 MB and 32 MB.
Software: All models are constructed by AutoCAD Release 12. Renderings and animation are made by 3D Studio Version 3.0 with touch-ups by PhotoShop 2.5 for Windows.

Notes: The effect of books on shelves was accomplished by using an image of book bindings as a texture map and B & W version of the same image as a transparency map. A similar technique was used to simulate the perforated metal of stair rails. The images of people were added by scanning posed photographs and splicing them in PhotoShop. Soft shadows were added in PhotoShop. Carpet and terrazzo textures were scanned from actual samples and touched-up in Photoshop to minimize "tile" effect. Terrazzo was given 25 percent reflectivity and carpets maps were made with 10 percent "bump" map.

Hellmuth, Obata + Kassabaum

Hardware: DEC 3100 VaxStation, 60 + 90 MHz Pentium, Silicon Graphics, Unix, Syquest Discs (Storage).
Software: HOK Draw (2D + 3D Data), HOK Image (Animation Set-up), HOK drawVision (2D + 3D Data Animation Set-up), Autodesk 3D Studio (3D Imagery; Animation), PAR CARD (Write Animation to VHS), Adobe PhotoShop (Photo Imagery), Adobe Illustrator (Illustration), Adobe Streamline (Bitmap Tracing), IMAGE Q (Computer Stills Presentation), Power Point (Computer Stills to Slides), Razor Pro (Video/Audio Editing), Render Print (36" x 120" Color Plots), HOK X-Animate (Animations), HOK Radiosity (Animation + Stills).
Input Device: Scanner, Video Capture Board (Digitize Footage from VHS or CamCorder).
Output Device: Canon Color Copier, HP 650c Large Format Color Plotter, Large Format B/W Electrostatic Plotter, 11 x 17-inch B/W Laser Copier,

Bohlin Cywinski Jackson Architects

Hardware: Quadra 950, 68040 chip at 50MHz. 400 MB of hard disk and 24 MB of RAM.
Software: Renderer package (and modeler) is ArchiCad by Graphisoft.

Notes: On average the images submitted took 1.5 to 2 hours to render.

ADD Inc

Hardware: Quadra 650 (28 MB RAM), 15-inch E-Machine color monitor, flatbed scanner, Bernoulli Removable Media, Zip Removable Media.
Software: Form Z, Infini-D, PowerDraw, AutoCAD R.12, Claris CAD, Strata StudioPro, Abobe PhotoShop, Fractal Painter, Aldus Freehand, HSC Bryce, OFOTO, POV-Ray.

Notes: Rendering times vary between six hours and three days.

Peter L. Gluck and Partners

Hardware: Silicon Graphics Indigo2 XL, R4400, 128 MB RAM.
Software: Integra tbt4.30, ARRIS, PhotoShop.

Technological Achievements in 3D Modeling
Mieczyslaw Boryslawski/View by View Inc.

Hardware: Macintosh: (5) Quadras 950 upgraded to Power PC with Apple Power PC upgrade cards, 2 Gig drives, 140 MB of RAM.
Silicon Graphics: Indigo II Extreme with RS 4400, 196 MB of RAM
Software: Macintosh: 3D modeling: Turbo 3D, FormZ and Amapi. 3D rendering and animation: Electric Image. Silicon Graphics: 3D rendering and animation: Lightscape.
Output Devices: Kodak XL 7700 dye sub printer, Kodak PCD 225 CD-ROM printer.

Digital Light and Space
Kent Larson

Hurva Synagogue Images
Hardware: Silicon Graphics Indigo2 XL, R4400, 128 MB RAM.
Software: Integra tbt4.30, ARRIS, PhotoShop.

Unity Temple Images
Hardware: Silicon Graphics Workstation.
Software: Lightscape Visualization System (Renderings), Arris (Modeling).

Historiography and Computer Renderings: A Reconstruction of the Josephine Baker House
Stephen Atkinson

Hardware: Silicon Graphics Personal Iris, Sun Workstations.
Software: Artisan, Adobe Photoshop.

Notes: Rendering time varied between 8 and 14 hours. Final images were touched-up using Adobe PhotoShop.

Cinematic Views of Architecture Through Computer Renderings
Richard Dubrow/Jon Kletzien /Advanced Media Design

Hardware: Various 486 PC computers with 32-64 MB RAM, Targa Plus video cards, Diaquest 422+ animation controller, Syquest 88 MB backup, Colorado jumbo 250 MB backup.
Software: Microsoft DOS v.5, Microsoft Windows v.3.1, Autodesk AutoCAD r.12, Autodesk Animator Pro, Autodesk 3D Studio r.2,3, and 4, Adobe PhotoShop for windows v.2.5, Ron Scott Hi Res Q Fx v.4, Diaquest Animaq-PC quick pass, Diaquest Action Animator, Yost Group IPAS plug-in #1, Schreiber Instruments Imagine Nursery, Digimation Lens-FX Ipas plug-in.
Input Device: MicroTek Scanmaker 2 scanner, Wacom drawing tablet, Ampex BVW-40 BetaCam video deck.
Output Device: Kodak XL 770 dye sublimation printer.

Notes: Advanced Media Design is a digital illustration and animation studio specializing in architectural representation. The staff strives to convey the client's design intent through the use of cutting edge media tools. The materials generated are often used for multiple presentations. Animation for the architectural client has been reused as the centerpiece of the fund-raising videos, architecture firms marketing videos, television news clips for public acceptance marketing, and printed for complementing written proposals.

Hyperrealism in Architectural Renderings
Michael Sechman

Hardware: PC-Based Computers.
Software: AutoCad (CAD), 3D Studio (Rendering), HiRes QFX (Image processing).
Output Device: Iris prints, 35mm slides, inkjet plotters.

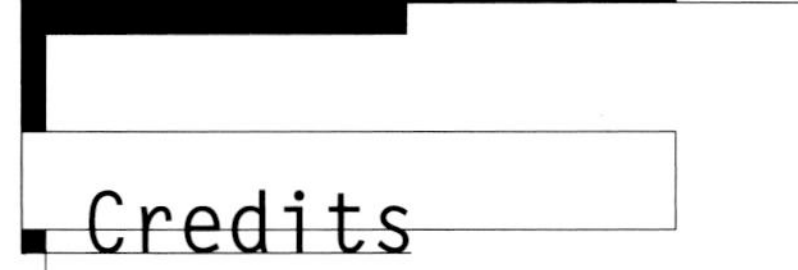

Credits

Just the Beginning of The Change

Saitama Arena, *Japan* (Page 6 and 7)
Arata Isozaki & Associates, Architects
CAD Center Corporation (Tokyo), Computer Renderings

Shanghai Stock Exchange, *Shanghai, China* (Page 8 and 9)
Kaplan McLaughlin Diaz, Architects
Michael Sechman, Computer Renderings

The Houston Project, *Houston, Texas* (Page 10 and 11)
Michael Bell, Architect
P. Quan, D. Marini, C. Nichols, Project Assistants

A.C.—after computer—Era

Agnes Etherington Art Centre, Competition Entry, *Ontario, Canada* (Page 12, Top)
A.J. Diamond, Donald Schmitt and Company, Architect
A.J. Diamond, Donald Schmitt and Company, 3D Model and Computer Rendering

IBM Canada Ltd., *Toronto, Canada* (Page 12, Bottom)
A.J. Diamond, Donald Schmitt and Company, Architect
A.J. Diamond, Donald Schmitt and Company, 3D Model and Computer Rendering

Faculty of Business Management, University of Toronto, Competition Entry, *Ontario, Canada* (Page 13, Top)
A.J. Diamond, Donald Schmitt and Company, Architect
A.J. Diamond, Donald Schmitt and Company, 3D Model and Computer Rendering

Jerusalem City Hall Complex, *Jerusalem, Israel* (Page 13, Bottom)
A.J. Diamond, Donald Schmitt and Company, Architect
A.J. Diamond, Donald Schmitt and Company, 3D Model and Computer Rendering

New Technologies, Lost Values

House in Richtfield, *Connecticut* (Page 14 and 16)
Kent Larson, Architect
Kent Larson, Computer Renderings

Kohn Pedersen Fox Associates PC

Greater Buffalo International Airport
Design Group: *A joint venture of Cannon, Kohn Pedersen Fox and William N. Bodouva & Associates*

Cannon
Mark Mendell, Managing Principal
David K. Macleod, Project Manager

Kohn Pedersen Fox
William Pedersen, Design Principal
A. E. Kohn, Managing Principal
Anthony Mosellie, Project Manager
Duncan Reid, Senior Designer
Philip Brown, Carey Chu, I. Ann Lin, Lucinda Dip, Kar-Wa Hoo, Bun-Wah Nip, Christopher Ernst, Brian Kaufman, Richard Clarke, Design Team
Advanced Media Design Inc., 3D Modeling and renderings

William N. Bodouva & Associates
William N. Bodouva, Principal
Sheldon Wander, Project Manager

Rafael Viñoly Architects

Yokohama International Airport Terminal
Raed Abilama ("SITE small" only), Ivo Kos, Michael Laviano (Image Manipulatiom for "EXT" also), Richard Schneebelli ("SITE small" only), Computer Renderings

Samsung Cultural Education and Entertainment Center
Wayne Herman, Ivo Kos, Iris Venado, Computer Renderings
Ivo Kos, Computer Renderings *(Video)*

Tokyo International Forum
Wayne Herman, Ivo Kos, Jonathan Schloss (Image Manipulation for TIF Montage), Computer Renderings
David Finn, Wayne Herman, Kinetic Designs, Ivo Kos, Felix Mendoza, Joe Pasquale, Video

Cesar Pelli & Associates

The Hague Tower
Cesar Pelli, Design Principal
Fred W. Clarke, Project Principal
William Butler, Design Team Leader
Jane Twombly, Philip Nelson, Hiro Shimizu, Designers
Philip Nelson, Computer Renderings

Del Bosque
Cesar Pelli, Design Principal
Fred W. Clarke, Project Principal
William Butler, Design Team Leader
Robert J. Espejo, Project Manager
Axel Zemborain, Karen Koenig, Lazarus Papanikolaou, Jane Twombly, Fritz Haeg, Jerome del Fierro, Designers
Philip Nelson, Axel Zemborain, Computer Renderings

Owens-Corning New World Headquarters
Cesar Pelli, Design Principal
Fred W. Clarke, Project Principal
Mark R. Shoemaker, Design Team Leader
Phillip G. Bernstein, Project Manager
Mihaly Turbucz, David Chen, Anne Haynes, Tetsushi Kadota, Karen Koenig, Julann Meyers, Philip Nelson, Dean Ober, Jane Twombly, Axel Zemborain, Designers
Philip Nelson, Axel Zemborain, Computer Renderings

Techint Corporate Headquarters
Cesar Pelli, Design Principal
Fred W. Clarke, Rafael Pelli, Project Principals
William Butler, Design Team Leader
Susana La Porta Drago, Project Manager
Philip Nelson, Jane Twombly, Roberto J. Espejo, Designers
Philip Nelson, Computer Renderings

One Market
Cesar Pelli, Design Principal
Fred W. Clarke, Project Principal
Turan Duda, Design Team Leader
Mariko Masuoka, John DaSilva, Robert Narracci, David Strong, Kristin Hawkins, Tim Paxton, Masaaki Ninomiya, Designers
Michael Sechman, Rob Narracci, Computer Renderings

Machado & Silvetti Associates

A New Entrance for Cranbrook
Rodolfo Machado, Jorge Silvetti, Project Designers
Peter Lofgren, Project Architect
Nader Tehrani, Project Coordinator
Beth Gibb, Mark Schatz, Project Team
Christopher Kirwan, Color Rendering
Stephen Atkinson, Franco Micucci, Francisco Thebaud, Model
Stephen Atkinson, Computer Renderings

Estudio Becker-Ferrari

The Tunnel
Alejandro Daniel Becker, General idea
Alejandro Daniel Becker, Claudio Ferrari, Project Designers
Alejandro Aisenson, Computer Renderings
Pablo Gallego, Rolando Pasarelli, Pablo Bernetich, Coordinators
Estacionamiento Plaza Italia S.A., Concessionary
Raffo y Mazzieres, General Contractor
Dr. Pablo Lopez Ruf, Legal Advisor

Office dA

Northeastern University Inter-Faith Chapel
Monica Ponce de Leon, Nader Tehrani, Project Designers
Erik Egbertson, Bent Karty, Computer Images *(Vector)*
Ben Karty, Computer Images *(Raster)*
Tim Dumbleton, Ben Karty, Animation
Jeffrey Asanza, Working Drawings *(Mylar Images)*
Yeong La, Model
Patricia Szu-Ping Chen, Dome Mock-up Model
Thamarit Suchart, Curtain Wall Mock-up Model
David Kunzig, Dana Manoliu, Salvatore Rafone, Rusty Walker, Project Team

Skidmore, Owings & Merrill

SOM/New York
Logan International Airport
David Childs, Design Partner
Scott Harrison, Marinha Mascheroni, Ken Lewis, Yangwei Yee, Don Fedorko, Renderers

Dulles International Airport Main Terminal Expansion
David Childs, Design Partner
Scott Harrison, David Martin, Renderer

Swiss Bank Corporation
David Childs, Design Partner
Maria Alataris, Renderer

SOM/Chicago
KAL Operations Center, Kimpo International Airport
Joseph Gonzalez, Design Partner
Scott Sarver, Renderer

Hong Kong Convention Centre
Larry Oltmanns, Design Partner
Marshall Strabala, Kamalrukh Katrak, Dan Ringlestein, Renderers

Aramco
Adrian Smith, Design Partner
Marshall Strabala, Larry Simerson, Dean Mamalakis, Renderers

Broadgate Development
Bruce Graham, Design Partner
Nate Kaiser, Michel Mossessian, Walt Bransford, Michael Gaffney, Pete Bochek, Renderers

World Trade Center
Michel Mossessian, Senior Designer
Nate Kaiser, Mark Allison, Andrew Myren, Steve Burns, Renderers

Jin Mao Building
Adrian Smith, Design Partner
Albert Anderson, Mark Schmieding, Nate Kaiser, Steve Hubbard, Renderers

SOM/San Francisco
101 Second Street
Craig Hartman, Design Partner
Ted Yoon, Renderer

San Francisco International Airport, Modernization Program
Craig Hartman, Design Partner
Peter Little, Leo Chow, Renderers

Gwathmey Siegel & Associates

The New York Public Library-Science, Industry & Business Library
Charles Gwathmey, Robert Siegel, Design principals
Jacob Alspector, Associate in charge
Earl Swisher, Project Architect
Sean Flynn, Job Captain
Elizabeth Skowronek, Computer Model
Elizabeth Skowronek, Computer Renderings
Rebecca Iovino, Photographs of People
Elizabeth Skowronek and Sean Chen (Icon Imaging Consortium), Photomontage
Rafael Castelblanco, Texture Maps for Books, Terrazzo and Perforated Metal

Master Plan Design Nanyang Polytechnic
Charles Gwathmey, Robert Siegel, Design principals
Joseph Ruocco, Associate in charge
Nelson Benavides, John Hunter, Jay Lampros, George Liaropoulos, Wei-Li Liu, Gregory A. Luhan, Frank Visconti, Project team
Nelson Benavides, John Hunter, Jay Lampros, George Liaropoulos, Wei-Li Liu, Gregory A. Luhan, Frank Visconti, Computer Model, Computer Renderings and Animation

Hellmuth, Obata + Kassabaum

Nanjing East Road Competition
Gyo Obata, Principal in Charge-Design
Ryan Stevens, Project Designer
Donald J. Fedorko, Computer Renderings

Fukuoka International Airport
William Valentine, Principal in Charge-Design
Steven Worthington, Project Designer
Michael Sechman, Computer Renderings

Hoffman-La Roche
Clark Davis, Principal in Charge
William Odell, Project Designer
David Munson, Computer Renderings

Société Générale
Daniel McCarthy, Project Designer
Dennis Belfiore, Project Manager
Donald Williams, Project Architect
David Munson, Computer Renderings

Salt Lake City Courts Complex
William Valentine, Principal in Charge-Design
Alan Bright, Project Designer
Michael Sechman, Computer Renderings

Bohlin Cywinski Jackson Architects

The Intelligent Workplace, Center for Building Performance & Diagnostics
The Center for Building Performance & Diagnostics, Carnegie Mellon University, Volker Hartkopf, Director, Vivian Loftness, Stephen Lee, AIA, Project Research & Development/Progamming
Pierre Zoelly, AIA, Zurich, Switzerland, Conceptual Design
Bohlin Cywinski Jackson, Architects of Record
Peter Q. Bohlin, FAIA, Jon C. Jackson, AIA, Robert S. Pfaffmann, AIA, Gregory R. Mottola, RA, Design Development & Documentation
R. M. Gensert & Associates, Inc. (Structural)
RAY Engineering, Inc. (Mechanical)
Hornfeck Engineering Company (Electrical), Consulting Engineers of Record
Representatives of the ABSIC Consortium, Peter A.D. Mill, Director, Centre of Building Diagnostics, Ottawa, Ardeshir Mahdavi, Carnegie Mellon Faculty, Advisors & Peer Review
Gregory R. Mottola, RA (Production CAD), Azizan Aziz, (Visualization CAD), Pierre Zoelly (thumbnail sketches), Binder Drawings
Azizan Aziz, Carnegie Mellon University, Electronic Renderings and Modeling

ADD Inc

66 Summer
Mark Glasser, Design Principal
Dave Fernandez, Senior Designer/Project Manager
Anna-Lisa Brown, Project Team
Anthony Tan, Computer Renderings

2 Devonshire
Mark Glasser, Design Principal
Eric Lambiaso, Senior Designer/Project Manager
Anthony Tan, Computer Renderings

Crosspoint
Wayne Koch, Design Principal
Steve Janeway, Senior Designer/Project Manager
Robert Del Savio, Julie Kim, Project Team
Anthony Tan, Computer Renderings

Boston Edison
Carolyn Hendrie, Design Principal
William Loftis, Senior Designer/Project Manager
Steve Janeway, Lisa Killaby, Eric Lambiaso, Emily Huang, Project Team
Anthony Tan, Computer Renderings

5 Cambridge Center
Wayne Koch, Design Principal
William Loftis, Senior Designer/Project Manager
Dave Fernandez, Vincenzo Giambertone, Gregory Kochanowski, Paul Matelic, Project Team
Anthony Tan, Computer Renderings

Peter L. Gluck & Partners

Pavilions and Pool at a Mies van der Rohe House
Kent Larson (Partner-in-charge), Peter L. Gluck, and Louis Turpin, Design Team
Kent Larson and Caleb Weisberg of Editel, NY, Computer Renderings

Private Sports Facility
Kent Larson (Partner-in-charge), Peter L. Gluck, David Craven, Gary Anderson, David Mansfield, Design Team
Kent Larson, Brenden Moran, Computer Renderings

Hitchcock Presbyterian Church
Kent Larson (Partner-in-charge), Peter L. Gluck, Phil Turino, Kelvin Ono, Design Team
Kent Larson, Brenden Moran, Computer Renderings

Synagogue in Scarsdale
Kent Larson (Partner-in-charge), Peter L. Gluck, Design Team
Kent Larson, Brenden Moran, Computer Renderings

Kellner Dileo Office
Kent Larson, (Partner-in-charge), Peter L. Gluck, Design Team
Kent Larson, Computer Renderings

Technological Achievements in 3D Modeling

San Jose Repertory Theatre, *San Jose, California* (Page 156)
Holt, Hinshaw, San Francisco, California, Architects
France Israel, 3D Model and Computer Renderings

Istanbul 2000 Olympic Bid, *Istanbul, Turkey* (Page 157)
Stang & Newdow, Atlanta, Georgia, Architects
Mieczyslaw Boryslawski, France Israel and Claire Schenenbeck, 3D Computer Model of the Olympic Park
Mieczyslaw Boryslawski and France Israel, Computer Rendering

University of California, San Francisco/Mount Zion Cancer Center, *San Francisco, California* (Page 158)
HGA, Minneapolis and ESS, San Francisco, Architects
Claire Schenenbeck and France Israel, 3D Computer Model
France Israel, Computer Rendering

The Kapiolani/Pikoi Towers, *Honolulu, Hawaii* (Page 159), *Claire Schenenbeck*, 3D Computer Model
France Israel, Computer Rendering

Yerba Buena Gardens, *San Francisco, California* (Page 160)
Mario Botta, Fumihico Maki, Stewart Polshek, Michell Giurgola, James Freed and Cesar Pelli, Architects
Mieczyslaw Boryslawski, France Israel and Claire Schenenbeck, 3D Computer Model
Mieczyslaw Boryslawski, France Israel, Computer Rendering

Yerba Buena Entertainment/Retail Complex, *San Francisco, California* (Page 161)
SMWM, San Francisco and Gary E. Handel Associates, New York, New York, Architects
France Israel, 3D Model and Computer Renderings

Digital Light and Space

Hurva Synagogue, *Jerusalem, Israel*, (1967) (Page 164-169)
Louis I. Kahn, Architect
Kent Larson, 3D Model and Computer Renderings

Unity Temple, *Oak Park, Illinois*, (1904) (Page 170-173)
Frank Lloyd Wright, Architect
Lightscape Technologies Inc., (San Jose, California), 3D Model and Computer Renderings

Historiography and Computer Renderings: A Reconstruction of the Josephine Baker House

Stephen Atkinson, Interior Renderings
David Lee and Stephen Atkinson, Exterior Renderings
David Lee, Animation Sequence

Cinematic Views of Architecture Through Computer Renderings

The Shanghai Business Center, *Shanghai, China* (Page 178)
Pei Cobb Freed Partners, Architects
H. Cobb, Principal in Charge
Advanced Media Design Inc. with Paul Stevenson Oles, FAIA, 3D Modeling and Renderings

The Hotel at the World Trade Center, *Boston, Massachusetts* (Page 179)
The Stubbins Associates, Architects
Richard Green, Principal in Charge
Advanced Media Design Inc, 3D Modeling and Renderings
Chris Leary (The Stubbins Associates), Additional 3D modeling

The Villa Savoye, *Poissy, France* (Page 180/181)
Le Corbusier, Architect
Advanced Media Design Inc., 3D Modeling, Rendering and Animation

Hyperrealism in Architectural Renderings

Capitol Towers, *Sacramento, California* (Page 182, Top and 186/187)
Kaplan McLaughlin Diaz, Architects
Michael Sechman, Computer Renderings

Indra Kayangan, *Kuala Lumpur, Malaysia* (Page 182, Bottom and 184/185)
ROMA, Architects
Michael Sechman, Computer Renderings

Far East International Building, *Shanghai, China* (Page 183)
Anshen and Allen, Architects
Michael Sechman, Computer Renderings

Dedication & Acknowledgments

To "Gran Pueblo Argentino Salud..." for being the primary source of my dreams, and to the people of the United States of America, for giving me the opportunity to make my dreams a reality.

Al "Gran Pueblo Argentino Salud..." por haber sido la fuente de mis sueños, y a los Estados Unidos de Norteamerica, por darme la posibilidad de realizarlos.

O.R.O.

I dedicate this book to my "definition of Father:" Hugo Luis Martinez Schettini, for being always just himself; and to my wife, Damaris, for her love and endless support.

Le dedico este libro a mi "definición de Padre:" Hugo Luis Martinez Schettini, por ser siempre él mismo; y a mi esposa, Damaris, por su amor e interminable apoyo.

L.H.G.

We would like to thank all the people whose criticism and support gave us good reasons to believe in the significance of making a book on this subject. Our main intention was to make a statement pre-announcing the enormous technological changes occurring in the architectural field. One of those changes, and the subject of this book, is the growth of computer technology that gives us the chance to visualize architecture in a more concrete and almost tangible reality.

It would have been impossible to present the contents of this book without the invaluable help of a selected group of professionals whose work is breaking preestablished notions of how architecture should be conceived and presented. From this outstanding group of professionals we would especially like to thank Kent Larson, Mieczyslaw Boryslawski, Stephen Atkinson, Richard Dubrow, Jon Kletzien, and Michael Sechman.

We would also like to acknowledge the endless support of Stuart Feldman, Crystal Son, Anthony Tan, Gretchen Bank, Yangwei Yee, Nader Tehrani, Monica Ponce de Leon, Janet Kagan, Philip Nelson, Elizabeth Skowronek, Daniel Becker, Michael Bell, Dana Collins, Gregory Mottola, David Gauld, Duncan Reid, and David Johnson.

Without the assistance of all of the above, it would have been impossible to make this book a reality.